Possessed
POSSESSIONS

Haunted antiques, furniture and collectibles

by
Ed Okonowicz

Possessed Possessions:
Haunted Antiques, Furniture and Collectibles
First Edition

Copyright 1996 by Edward M. Okonowicz Jr.
All rights reserved.

ISBN 0-9643244-5-8

Published by
Myst and Lace Publishers
1386 Fair Hill Lane
Elkton, Maryland 21921

Printed in the U.S.A.
by Cedar Tree Press

Typography and Design
by Kathleen Okonowicz

Dedications

To my Dad, who took me by the hand and
showed me how to appreciate the unusual.
Ed Okonowicz

To my grandparents, Ken and Katie Buker,
who I miss ever so much.
Kathleen Burgoon Okonowicz

Acknowledgments

The author and illustrator appreciate the assistance of those
who have played an important role in this project.

Special thanks are extended to:

Kathlene Stegura
for her technical expertise;

John Brennan
Sue Moncure,
Ted Stegura and
Monica Witkowski
for their proofreading and suggestions;

Don Johnson, for his articles about this book;

and, of course,

particular appreciation to the ghosts and their hosts.

Also available from
Myst and Lace Publishers

Spirits Between the Bays Series

Volume I
Pulling Back the Curtain
(October, 1994)

Volume II
Opening the Door
(March, 1995)

Volume III
Welcome Inn
(September, 1995)

Volume IV
In the Vestibule
(Fall, 1996)

Stairway over the Brandywine
A Love Story
(February, 1995)

Possessed Possessions:
Haunted Antiques, Furniture and Collectibles
(Spring, 1996)

Table of Contents

TRUE STORIES

The Troubled Doll*   6
Aberdeen, Maryland

Goblins in the Mirror*   13
Hanover, Pennsylvania

Grandfather's Two Favorites*   16
Bear, Delaware

The Sea Captain's Dresser   20
Baltimore, Maryland

Invisible Lamplighter   25
Wahalla, South Carolina

The Haunted Headboard*   28
Arbutus, Maryland

The Jade Ring*   32
West Chester, Ohio

Unframed in Maine   36
Bangor, Maine

Old Hotel Washstand   41
Clarington, Pennsylvania

Portal in the Glass   45
Central Ohio

Jonathan's Special Chair*   47
Western Shore of Maryland

Don't Open the Trunk   56
  Coatesville, Pennsylvania

Gingerbread Clock   59
  Laura, Ohio

The Upside-Down Rocker*   61
  South Paris, Maine

Things that Go Pop in the Night. . . and Day   64
  Goldsboro, Maryland

The Mysterious Victrola   71
  Hagerstown, Maryland

Unsettling Margaret   75
  Bricktown, New Jersey

The Cursed Desk*   79
  Gainesville, Florida

Where There's Smoke There's . . . a Ghost   84
  Hartford, Wisconsin

The Antique Copper Bathtub*   87
  Pulaski, Tennessee

All of the stories in this section of the book are true and all of them are based upon interviews with those who have experienced unusual events. However, the individuals in the stories designated with ✤ have requested that their actual names not be used.

Legend and Lore

The Anniversary Ring   91
  Elkton, Maryland

*Many of the stories in this volume were received from people in the Eastern U.S. Stories from this and other parts of the country will be featured in future volumes. Please see page 104 for information about **Possessed Possessions 2** and how to share your story.*

Introduction

hosts. Phantoms. Spirits. Poltergeists. Wraiths. Little People. No matter what they are called, these citizens of the beyond have fascinated mystics and magicians, preachers and psychics, skeptics and believers since the beginning of time.

From campfire tales to academic dissertations, stories of the antics of restless spirits are both a source of frightening entertainment and the focus of serious research.

No one knows for sure why certain souls refuse to pass on and live happily (or unhappily) ever after. Neither are we able to determine why some of the living seem to possess an advanced level of psychic ability and are more sensitive than others in encountering or observing the unexplained.

Many cultures believe that spirits remain on Earth after the body has been put to rest because of unfinished business that must be addressed, or because the death was the result of a sudden, horrifying experience.

But, I began to wonder:

• Why should the wanderings of these doomed stragglers be limited to stuffy museums, or damp, decrepit buildings or lonely fields?

• And why must they be forced to pass their never-ending time in the form of a cloaked specter or a white-sheeted friend of Casper?

• What is to stop them from taking up residence in personally precious items that were significant to them during the days when they were rightfully out and about?

About the objects

Like Aladdin's "Genie in the Bottle," perhaps some ghosts feel more comfortable resting within an intricately hand-carved, 19th-century chair, inside a piece of hand-made, heirloom jewelry or in the scabbard of a pirate's secret dagger. Others, meanwhile, may select their eternal home within the bosom of a delicate, porcelain doll, behind the smooth, reflective surface of an ornate Victorian mirror or inside the pitted rock of an ancient, molded sculpture.

Hold a Revolutionary-era musket ball in your hand and you might wonder where it was made, when it was fired and, just perhaps, whose body it passed through.

Is that rust on the old cavalry soldier's sword?

Maybe it's a fleck of dried blood that has been affixed to the metal since it was run through a young, 16-year-old Johnny Reb charging upon the Union lines at Shilo.

Is it possible that the soul of the subject of that morose, 18th-century portrait still exists—in some unexplained way, on some unknown level—behind the painted eyes that gaze upon all who pass beneath the dead man's curious stare.

What stories have these ancient objects kept to themselves . . . or may now be trying to share?

In the beginning

This *objective* quest began by accident. While seeking true ghost stories on the Delmarva Peninsula for the **Spirits Between the Bays** series, I met John Klisavage, an interesting antique dealer in Havre de Grace, Maryland.

It was during a conversation in his rare books and antiques shop in that historic community that he shared stories he has heard about "haunted" objects.

Afterwards, I wondered if other restless items, curious curios and active antiques had tales to tell. I began asking questions of other dealers and collectors about the possibility of things that were seemingly "haunted" or "possessed."

In the beginning, leads were few. That first dealer helped me contact another, who shared a story. Eventually, the mysterious mirror owner led me to the agitated dresser's keeper, who suggested the custodian of the haunted headboard.

2

Slowly, I found others who owned possessed objects. Later, news stories announced my search for haunted objects in regional and national antique newspapers, including *Antique Week*, *Antique Trader Weekly*, *Antiques West* and *Maine Antique Digest*.

The immediate response by phone and through the mail was more than I had imagined. Like a thin line in a game of connect the dots, ***Possessed Possessions: Haunted Antiques, Furniture and Collectibles*** began to take shape.

Through interviews and visits, I discovered that some possessions do indeed have intriguing pasts, and each object's characteristics and actions depend upon its use, purpose and history.

A few of the items I discovered were made specifically for supernatural rituals and mysterious ceremonies. Most, however, were everyday objects designed for normal household use. Some resided in stately mansions and were well cared for. Others were exposed to the underbelly of life and survived amongst a soap opera of pain and suffering.

In these cases, the powerful energy that accompanies sudden tragedies and life's stacked deck of disappointments seems to have rubbed off. Some believe these complex emotions can be transmitted to an object and remain within the piece for decades, even centuries.

Nothing but the Truth

The incidents in this book are real. They are reported exactly as they were told to me. They are not the product of the author's imagination, but the result of contact and discussion with average people who work, play and raise families.

This book does not attempt to solve the mysteries about why these items are possessed; it simply relates unusual and unexplainable stories about objects that have refused to give up the ghost.

In fact, these tales present more questions than answers.

In sharing their tales, most of troubled objects' owners have admitted they wonder:

What is going on?

How can these things happen? and

Why was I chosen to be a frustrated and frightened victim?

According to John Sikorski, host of "Sikorski's Attic"—a one-hour, call-in radio talk show about antiques and collectibles originating from public radio affiliate WUFT-FM in Gainesville, Fla.—"Many people today are into collecting for the short-term profits they can realize. Less are involved in collecting because of their special interest, attachment or love of certain objects."

Perhaps, applying John's comment, objects—that once were loved because of their beauty, quality workmanship and the pride of long-term family ownership—are now held in unfamiliar settings and considered nothing more than short-term investments to be disposed of to the highest bidder when the market is right.

In such cases, these objects may miss the former owners who thought of them differently, and the items may be trying to send out calls for help, or gain the current owner's attention.

John offered another comment, one quite interesting that both novice and serious antique hunters are sure to understand: He said collectors often will use the phrase "It just didn't speak to me," after exiting an antique sale empty handed.

Others, meanwhile, might say, "It jumped out at me," trying to explain why they purchased a particular item from among thousands of choices.

"Something about it stops you," John said, "and you see it. It's caught your attention. You may even pick it up and may not be sure as to why."

Obviously, something has attracted the buyer to the item. But who is to know whether it is a keen eye, a sixth sense, a hunch about the potential for future profit or a summons that originated from an eerie dimension beyond our mortal understanding.

The search continues

No one has final, foolproof answers. Even experts can only offer opinions or educated guesses.

As a group, the bedeviled caretakers can at least take comfort in knowing they are not alone, that there definitely are others who remain confused from bizarre events traced to an object.

While I express my thanks and deepest appreciation to those who provided these initial stories, I invite others in the business of searching, selling and collecting antiques, objects and furniture to contact me about their own experiences or with tales they may have heard.

As a result of my recent hunt in the wonderfully confusing world of antiques, I suggest you be wary of that special piece that now stands unattended—patiently awaiting its resurrection from the locked trunk in your garage or from the cardboard box in the back of your cluttered van. Keep in mind that the object you now own may host the restless soul of some agitated spirit.

And when the phantom finally makes its need for attention known to you—possibly in the wee small hours of some mist-shrouded morning—please, I beseech you, don't hesitate to call us and share your tale. For we all are interested in reading about it in the next volume of this series.

Until we meet again in ***Possessed Possessions 2*** . . .

Happy Hauntings and Good Luck in Your *Collecting*,

—Ed Okonowicz
in Fair Hill, Maryland,
at the northern edge of
the Delmarva Peninsula
—Spring 1996

The Troubled Doll

It was a bright Sunday morning when Chuck Palmer welcomed me into his home in Aberdeen, Maryland. The neat, single-story residence contained many interesting antiques and collectibles that he had gathered over several years.

Chuck explained that he worked for a company that handled the administration and maintenance of hundreds of rental units, ranging in size from small apartments to large houses. Being in the clean-up end of the business, Chuck said he was involved in clearing out a lot of the residences when renters took off without notice.

His employers said he could keep whatever he wanted and throw the rest of the stuff away. At times, he came across what he considered to be worthwhile items, ranging from usable furniture to smaller knickknacks. He would keep some of these objects for his personal collections. If others seemed interesting, he might offer them to antique dealers in some of the small nearby towns.

At 47, he was trim, healthy and, on this particular day, very willing to share his most unusual story with someone who didn't look at him as if he had three eyes.

The subject of our conversation was a doll. "The doll" is the way he referred to it. It didn't have a name, he said, but the mysterious object was well known to him, his wife, children and relatives.

"Let's get down to it!" Chuck said, eager to begin. A cigarette in his hand, he was sitting on a tall stool near his kitchen counter.

In rapid-fire bursts, he spun out an amazing tale that he had shared with less than a half dozen people over the five-year period since the doll—and a series of strange incidents—came into his life.

"First, let me tell you, I'm an ex-Marine, a Vietnam combat veteran and an average sensible person. I believe there is a simple solution to everything." Then, taking a drag on his smoke, he added, shaking his head, "Apparently, that's not the case this time."

In 1989, Chuck explained, he and his wife, Kathy, would make the rounds of yard sales regularly.

"We like to prowl Havre de Grace," he added, referring to the watertown on the western shore of the Susquehanna River, at the edge of Harford County, Md. "It's antique row up there. We went into a small shop and saw a doll, settin' on a table."

He described it as about 18 inches high and dressed in a full, white wedding-style gown. The garments were obviously carefully handmade of white silk and lace material. The couple inquired about the price, expecting it to be at least $100.

"When she said $10," Chuck recalled, "I said to myself, *My God! There's more than that much in the silk of the dress.* Kathy bought it right away. She couldn't believe the price."

When they got the doll home, they saw that its feet had been nailed into a small block of wood, which had been wrapped in the same white material as the dress.

Kathy was pleased with her bargain and placed the doll on top of the television set. Chuck said she considered it a centerpiece in the living room of their single-family, frame house that had been built in the 1930s.

"A few days later," Chuck said, thinking back to when the activity started, "our 14-year-old daughter, Susan, said that she thought the doll's eyes were following her when she walked through the room."

Taking another puff from his cigarette and shaking his head, Chuck smiled. "I remember that I went up to it. Looked at it real close. The way the eyes were set, they looked like glass. I figured it could appear to be that way. But I also knew kids, with their imaginations. So I never paid much attention to it."

Later, when Susan got home from school, and only she and her brother were in the house, she said she would hear the sound of someone roller skating in the hallway.

"I passed that off, too," said Chuck. "But then, our son, Ricky, who was about 9, said he heard the skates, and he also saw the doorknobs turning, all by themselves. I still didn't realize what was happening."

A few weeks later, Kathy tried to set the doll on the bed, but it kept falling over. She asked Chuck to remove the block of wood from the doll's feet.

"I tell you, thinking back on it now," he said, "I didn't feel right about taking the block of wood off. But, the doll seemed to fit in there real nice, sat real comfortable on the bed."

It was in the evening, a few nights later, when Chuck was walking down the hallway, toward the bedroom, and saw the doorknob turning on the door to the room that held the doll.

"*This is ridiculous*, I remember saying to myself. I'm looking for a simple, common sense cause. I opened the door and there was no one there, only the doll sittin' on the center of the bed."

After that small, unexplained appetizer, Chuck was confronted with the main-course attention grabber.

Kathy's mother was visiting one weekend. It was a Saturday night, about 10 o'clock, and Chuck told the two women, who were talking in the kitchen, that he was going to turn in for the evening.

As was the couple's custom, he took the doll from her spot on the bed and placed it in a corner of the room.

"She was settin' in the corner... and there was a light, more like a glow, but she looked fleshy. Like she was real."

"Now, I'm sure not more than one minute had passed, maybe not even that long," Chuck stressed. "I had just put my head on the pillow, when I heard a rustling noise. I thought it was a mouse.

"I turned to see a little girl. I had to raise my body to get a good look. And it was a little girl, about 5 years old. She had blond hair, parted completely in the middle, and cut high in the front and back.

"She was settin' in the corner, only 10 feet away, and there was a light, more like a glow, but she looked fleshy. Like she was real. She was there for a few seconds. Just settin' there, rockin' with the doll."

Chuck said he grabbed his clothes and got dressed on the run.

"I shot out of that door. Damn right I did! I got into

the kitchen and told them I saw a little girl back there. When we got into the room, she made a liar out of me. There was nothing but the doll, and they didn't believe me.

"I tell you, when I went back in there later I turned the light on. And I remember telling Kathy, 'I don't think we shoulda taken that block of wood off the doll.' "

After that, Chuck said he and Kathy started looking at all the things they had brought into the house, trying to see if there was something—other than the doll—that might be the cause of the procession of strange events.

After a few weeks they couldn't isolate the cause, but during that time they did sell a lot of the stuff. But, for some reason, they did not sell the doll.

The obvious question was asked: Why not?

Chuck just shook his head and softly said, "I don't know."

Eventually, they moved to a different house nearby. The doll took up its usual place on the center of the bed. "Toby," a Dalmatian about 10 years old, had its favorite place under the bed.

Chuck noticed that as long as the doll was in the bedroom, Toby would never enter the room.

"We tried to coax it, but it wouldn't come in," Chuck recalled. "Then the roller skates started again. But, this time, I'm not going to say they're imagining anything, not after what I'd seen."

It was about 8 in the evening and Kathy was standing in front of a mirror, getting dressed and putting on a pair of earrings. To her right side, about five feet away, a wind-up baby swing was in a collapsed state and leaning against an overstuffed chair. Behind the swing, and on the cushion of the chair, sat the doll.

The swing was angled, pointing away from Kathy and toward the chair and the face of the doll.

Chuck, who was walking down the hallway toward the bedroom, could see Kathy directly through the open door. To his shock, and Kathy's, the swing flew up and slammed into his wife's side, hitting her hard enough to leave a blackish bruise.

"It left the chair. It just got up on its own legs and hit her in the side," Chuck said, still amazed at what he saw several years ago. "There was no way a baby swing, lying against a chair, could get up and fly five feet in the air and leave a bruise. It's impossible!

"Kathy said, 'That damn doll is jealous. It doesn't want another woman in the house! I want that thing out of here!'"

Chuck recalled his reply. "I'm not taking it outta the house tonight, because it's dark!"

So he compromised by putting the doll temporarily inside a large, empty dome-topped trunk that stood at the foot of the bed. He then locked the top.

Later, when they were lying in bed, they both saw a small, bright, white light leave the trunk and float up toward the ceiling of the room. After traveling around the walls of their bedroom, it ended up in a far corner, made a popping sound, then disappeared.

With the doll in the trunk, several days passed and things were calm. Chuck said they all thought the worst had passed and they were rid of any problems. Until . . .

Until Chuck saw the ashtray on his night stand start rocking and spinning. He waited for it to stop, then he felt his body being pushed up and down, from underneath him. It was as if something was forcing the center of his body, in the area of the small of his back, to leave the bed and drop, several times in repetition.

"Hellfire! It's after midnight, and I'm 160 pounds, and I'm going up and down in the bed. Something was pushing me up and down. Now I do have to tell you, it felt relaxing. There was nobody under the bed, I knew that, but I looked anyway.

"That did it for me. When daylight came, I said, 'That doll is outta here!' I took it outta the trunk, put her in a green, plastic garbage bag and took her to Tim's, our son's house."

Chuck said he left the doll at his boy's and didn't have any problems for six months. Like others in the family, Tim was fully aware of his parent's haunted doll situation.

One evening, while looking at the doll that was still at his place, Tim, who was six feet tall and 190 pounds, asked his father what he was going to do with the troublemaker.

"I told him, 'I guess I'm going to get rid of it,'" Chuck said. "And the lights flashed on and off, like somebody was saying: 'NO!' There was no power failure outside, we looked. We both stared at each other and tried to ignore it. Then Tim said, 'Are you sure you should get rid of it?'

"The lights went out completely. Hellfire! We both went through the door and he was out of the house before I was. That was four years ago, and since then she's been out in the shed in a green leaf bag and I ain't had a problem. It only seems to occur when it's in a house."

Chuck walked into his yard and opened the shed door. He pulled out a large dark plastic bag. He explained that he had gone out back the day before, to make sure it was there for me to see when I arrived.

"I was afraid to get rid of it after the lights," he said.

Obviously unsure of what to do, he said, "I figured I would leave it where it is until I decide what to do with it. My son, he doesn't want it. Kathy doesn't want it."

Spreading open the bag, he revealed the feared object. The inside of the green plastic bag was filled with white material. Chuck grabbed the doll by the feet and pulled it out into the sunlight—its first encounter in four years with a world beyond lawnmowers, old furniture and storage supplies.

Surprisingly, it wasn't a delicate porcelain antique. Rather, it was like an oversized Barbie. But, it's hair was short and dark brown, with patches of a lighter color, as if it had been frosted in sections.

"It's a modern doll," he said, as if he was reading my mind. "That's what makes it so peculiar. She sort of looks to me like a Barbie."

It was the eyes, however, that pulled one's attention. They were almost real—dark blue—with heavy blue eye shadow all around them. The lashes were long, almost life-like. One could understand how the children thought it might be staring at them, watching as they passed.

The dress was made of white silk, lots of it. Certainly a wedding dress or formal attire, and the top from the waist to the neck, was white lace.

Underneath the mass of material, it wore only one yellow shoe, the other lost long ago. Through the top of each foot was a hole that protruded into the sole, a permanent reminder of where the nails had been driven that secured the feet to the block of wood.

Having heard the stories that Chuck had been willing to share, I was careful to let him handle the flesh-colored, rubber, lifelike creature. My curiosity satisfied, he replaced the silent little lady deep in her dark green plastic tomb. After twisting the thin wire tie, Chuck took the bag and disappeared into the lonely darkness, placing his possession in the farthest corner of the shed. He came out, closed the door, snapped the padlock and offered a quick smile, saying, "That'll hold her . . . I hope."

We both let out a weak laugh.

Back in the house, he reflected on the bizarre succession of events that he had experienced, but that seem so strange and impossible to others.

"I would always try to apply common sense," he said. "I would have to see it to believe it. I thought if we use reasonable logic we should be able to find answers, if we look hard enough.

"I tell you, I wouldn't believe it if somebody told me. I would have to see it for myself. But what happened is what you got from me today, right here. Cut out all the bull and the imagination. You've got the truth. I could have told you cups and saucers were flying around the room, but that didn't happen. You got just the facts. There's nothing extra added, nothing deleted."

Chuck said he never went back to see the woman who sold him the doll. But he believes she knew something about it, especially since she sold it so cheaply.

While the facts of Chuck's story are interesting, his thoughts on why it happened show he's spent a considerable amount of time trying to answer the questions: *Why did all this happen?* and *What should he have done, or be doing?*

"I wonder sometimes," Chuck said, "did it want something, was there something we were supposed to do? How are we supposed to communicate with it? I know that may sound ridiculous, but the lights going on and off, it was as if it said, 'No! You're not going to get rid of me!' I even wonder sometimes if it's comfortable in the shed. It sounds crazy; after all, it's an inanimate object.

"Sometimes I think it was telling me, 'No! I don't want to go.' If I knew what to do for it, within reason, to give it peace, I would do it. But it doesn't talk. It doesn't write notes."

12

Goblins in the Mirror

anover, Pennsylvania, southeast of Gettysburg, is one of those old, mid-Atlantic country towns with a central business district rapidly being surrounded by an expanding circle of suburban developments and shopping malls.

But, if you travel the back roads toward the famous battlefield town to the north, you can catch fleeting glimpses of the past, a troubled time more than 130 years ago when Blue fought Gray in a battle many consider the turning point of the War Between the States.

"A lot happened here," Tillie said, "probably because this whole area was involved in the Civil War battle."

The Hanover wife and mother was carefully setting the scene for the story she was about to tell, a tale so strange and troubling that her daughter would not discuss the events she had experienced. In fact, Tillie said, the younger girl had blocked many of the horrifying incidents from her mind.

Several years ago, Tillie explained, when her daughter was 18 years old, she and a roommate moved into a small apartment. It was located in the center of town, above an old general store. There had been rumors that ghosts roamed the building. But, Tillie said, there was hardly an old structure in Hanover whose owners didn't claim to have a few restless spirits.

"We helped Paige move in. Soon afterward we bought her an antique dresser," Tillie said.

The piece was about 50 years old, and the wood was a light blond color. It had several drawers and was built low enough to support a large mirror that filled the area above the dresser's wide, flat top.

"When you looked into the mirror the reflection was distorted," said Tillie. "Your image was odd, not clear. Even when you moved from side to side, the view was never completely right. One time, when I was visiting, I actually thought I saw a small red light in the mirror. It seemed as if it was coming from way in the back. But I thought I was crazy."

Several strange things seemed to occur in both the apartment and the hall entrance that came up the enclosed, narrow set of stairs from the street-level, exterior door.

Once, Paige and her friend awoke in early morning darkness to find a young girl sitting at the foot of Paige's bed. Apparently the small unexpected guest was trying to talk to the two roommates. They could see the child clearly, and her mouth was moving, but neither girl could hear anything. The same little girl, dressed in 1920s-style clothing, also appeared on the stairs and was seen by several other family members who happened to be visiting at the time.

Paige's first experience with the mirror occurred when she was sitting on the foot of her bed, gazing across the room at her distorted image in the old glass.

Suddenly, she stopped combing her hair, walked slowly toward the glass surface and began to focus far into the depths of the mirror. Leaning over the top of the dresser, she moved closer to the glass surface.

It was then that she saw a horrifying face, very tiny and distant. Paige pressed her face against the reflective glass, to get as close as possible to the surface to get a better look at the creature.

As the figure began to come into focus, Paige noticed that there were no longer glowing eyes in the sockets of the face . . . only a pair of deep black holes that formed two, tiny dots of inky blackness.

"She told us about it," Tillie said. "She also said she saw some kind of a demon in the mirror. We never questioned her. We believed her. She was never one to make things up for the sake of attention.

"We began to worry when Paige broke out in a horrible rash," Tillie said. "It was all over her body. Sometimes, she actually took the mirror off the back of the dresser and kept it out of view, behind the dresser. Then, there was the phone call. That was horrifying for all of us."

Tillie said Paige called her and was hysterical on the other end of the line. She was shouting, begging her mother to come to the apartment, saying there was something in the room and that the demons were trying to get her.

Tillie drove like a wild woman. Arriving at the old building, she took the steps two at a time and found her daughter huddled at the doorway of the apartment, shaking and sobbing.

"She was out of control," Tillie said. "She was shouting, 'Don't go back into the bedroom! It's still there! It's going to get all of us. It will get you, too!'"

Tillie moved her daughter aside, went down the apartment's short hallway and opened the bedroom door.

Immediately, Paige raced in from behind.

"She passed in front of me and started twirling, spinning around, like she was possessed," Tillie said. "Her head jerked back and her eyes rolled up toward the top of her head. She was spinning around in circles, very fast.

"My heart was pounding. I actually saw her starting to rise off the floor, as if something was pulling her up into the air. I was afraid she was going to be dropped, or fall and hit her head against a piece of furniture. I pulled her out of there and took her home with me."

Tillie and Paige's roommate got rid of the dresser within days.

Today, nearly a decade later, her daughter doesn't remember much of that horrifying period. "Or, if she does," Tillie said, "she won't talk about it.

"She passed in front of me and started twirling, spinning around, like she was possessed."

"I believe all this is possible. I think the unexplained does happen. I saw the red light appear in the mirror once. It was in the morning. But I feel that all of this was caused by someone who had died in the building and I figure that the restless spirit was still around.

"After Paige left that apartment, I often wanted to go back and ask the new people who lived there if anything happened. But I never did."

Grandfather's Two Favorites

illy Peaches still can't remember when he first noticed strange things start to happen, probably because he was drunk at the time. In those years, when he would be laid off from his construction job, he was nursing a buzz quite a lot.

He and his wife, Margie, lived in an old bungalow in a development that was on the decline, in Bear, just outside Wilmington, Delaware. The grass on many of the lots was high. Cars that didn't run anymore decorated quite a few front yards. They rested like rusted, modern sculpture, their headlights peeking out at the curb through clumps of tall weeds.

Margie and Billy had only been married about a year, but they hadn't been getting along for several months. Things were going downhill fast. Every time an argument got past the point of no return, Margie would begin throwing things— plates, silverware, anything that was within her reach.

On this early Sunday morning, she made the mistake of picking up one of Billy's hand-painted eagles and threw it across the bedroom. The wooden piece, that had taken him more than 20 hours to make, splintered into a dozen pieces.

"I lost it, man," he said, shaking his head, thinking back at the incident that had occurred nearly 10 years earlier. "It was like my mind snapped," Billy added. "I charged straight at her.

"She ran down the hallway, into the dinin' room and started pushing chairs at me, to slow me down. But I tossed them aside and started to climb over the table toward her. It was then . . . . Look, you're going to think this sounds crazy, but, I swear, while I was on top of the table, trying to get across, the damn thing starts liftin' up in the air. With me on top, it's movin' me up to the ceiling."

Billy said he just froze on all fours and didn't move. Within seconds, as total amazement replaced his fury, the table lowered itself to the floor.

Margie, holding her hands to her mouth in fear, had pushed herself back up against the dining room wall, trying to get as far away as possible from what she didn't believe was actually happening.

After he jumped off the table, Billy said he ran behind the kitchen counter.

"Nobody said nothin' after that," Billy said. "Margie just went into the other room and turned on the TV. And me, I went into the bedroom and finished off what was left in an old fifth of Southern Comfort, and I fell off to sleep."

The next day, neither Billy or Margie mentioned the rising table.

At the time, he thought because he was drunk and in a rage, that he had imagined the incident. He never asked his wife her opinion.

"I didn't want her to think I was nuts, if it didn't happen," Billy said, "or think I was bothered by it, if it did."

About a week later the couple had another rouser of a fight. They were both throwing things and chasing each other around the house.

"Every time she ran into the dining room, the doors on the wall cabinets in the kitchen would start slamming back and forth, like somebody was in there pullin' them open then smashin' them closed real hard. I thought the damn things were going to break from the force.

"As I stopped to look at what was happenin', one of the chairs, from beside the table, slid across the floor and hit me down here, right where it hurts, ya know," Billy was pointing toward his groin. "I know what you're thinkin', that I'm nuts. But I'm not makin' this up."

Margie, Billy explained, was at the opposite end of the room and could not have hit him with the chair. Bent over in pain, he grabbed the chair and tossed it into the air. He heard a leg, or some part of it, crack when it hit the living room wall.

"The next mornin', I checked the chair that I threw. It was on the floor where it landed after I tossed it. It was fine.

There was no crack, nothing wrong with it. Not even a scratch."

When the couple was calm and relaxed, about midweek, Billy and Margie sat at the dining room table and discussed what had happened. Not surprisingly, they had different opinions and Margie denied anything had happened. True to form, Billy started yelling at his wife, telling her she was stupid.

"That's when the kitchen cabinet doors slammed shut again, all by themselves. It was two loud smashes. She heard it, too. I said, 'You think I'm crazy now?' She was speechless and sat there shivering, like she was freezing with the chills. I thought she was goin' to go beserko."

As weeks went by, Billy said the only time he heard the smashing cabinets or saw any more movement from the dining room table was when he and Margie were having an argument.

"At first, the weird stuff happened when we were really goin' at it. Soon, though, it got to the point were I couldn't even raise my voice or a door would smash. And if we were fightin' anywhere near the dinin' room, a chair would come flyin' at me. I even stopped goin' in the damn room. Sat in the kitchen or livin' room and ate all my meals on the couch."

"...if we were fightin' anywhere near the dinin' room, a chair would come flyin' at me. I even stopped goin' in the damn room."

Margie told her mother about the strange happenings and the fighting and deterioration of the marriage. The older woman called a few days later and said she had arranged for a psychic to visit Margie's home.

The visitation occurred early one evening when Billy and Margie were present and on their best behavior.

The psychic walked through the house and said she could feel the presence of tension. Things were not pleasant. Everyone seemed ill at ease.

Billy said he was uncomfortable. He didn't know what from the past the woman could see or what she knew about their problems.

"It wasn't no pleasant experience," he said, "sittin' there thinkin' someone might be able to see the fights we had.

"Near the end of her visit, she asked us where we got the dinin' room furniture. Margie told her it was from her grandfather. Then the lady asked a few more questions: 'Was Margie close to her grandfather? Did she love him? Miss him?'

"My wife and her grandfather were real close. He didn't have much, but told everybody, every time the family had a picnic or party, that: 'My little Margie is to get my dining room set when I die. Be sure that happens or I'll come back and haunt all of ya.'

"It became like a family joke, the old man said it so often. When the psychic brought him up, the whole thing was so obvious we should have thought of it ourselves."

The psychic said she definitely felt the presence of an older man. He was there to protect Margie. He was going to stay as long as necessary. She could not convince him to leave and go to rest. The grandfather was using his dining room set to defend his favorite granddaughter.

It wasn't long after that strange meeting that Billy moved out. The couple split up, another marriage had hit the rocks and broken into thousands of painful pieces.

As for the possessions?

"We didn't have much to split up," Billy said. "I got the stereo, tapes, some bedroom furniture." Then, offering a tight grin, he added, "I guess you figured out that she took the dinin' room. No way I wanted any part of that crap.

"She's still got it with her, I guess. But, I tell you this, if I ever run into her again, I know I'm going to ask the guy she's with if he's met grandpa yet. Bet that will get a rise outta her."

Sea Captain's Dresser

usan Levin's father owned a neighborhood bar on Howard Street in Baltimore. The building was a hangout and home away from home for a steady clientele who were more like family than customers.

Some of the regulars were always ordering drinks but unable to pay. So they would run up a tab. "Put it on the book," they'd said, promising to pay the house back what they owed from their next paycheck, when their ship came in, when their number hit, when their horse crossed the line at Pimlico or . . . when they remembered.

So, instead of cold, hard cash (which he preferred), Susan's father often ended up with beat-up pocket watches (a drawer full of them), assorted rings (lots of interesting rings) and lighters (plenty of Zippos with other people's initials). Then, there were different kinds of musical instruments, cameras, costume jewelry and radios—all collecting dust in the back storage room, waiting to be redeemed, sold or given away.

But it was the furniture that caused quite a stir, not at the bar, but at Susan's home, where her father had it delivered.

"The stuff is too big to get up through those stairs to the rooms above the bar," he told Susan and her mother, so he had a few of the regulars with access to a pickup drop the assorted pieces off at their home on Beechfield Avenue.

The neat row house, on the southwest side of the city, was built about 90 years ago on land that had once been part of an old estate. The original mansion still stands on Cedar Garden Street, Susan said.

"There always was something strange about that house," Susan recalled. Now in her mid 40s, she lives in the

Catonsville area, but said she can clearly recall many of the unusual incidents that occurred during her teenage years.

"So many things happened, especially to me and my mother. I heard talking, touched things—like human bones—and experienced other souls who were present in our house, but you couldn't see them there."

The first experience occurred when Susan was 17 years old. She turned over in bed one night and saw a figure that she thought was her mother. But she realized it had no face. All she could see was long brown hair, a green dress and a glowing presence.

Three years later, Susan's mother saw the same apparition in the living room.

"My mother heard a creaking sound behind her," Susan said. "She turned and there was the woman with long brown hair and the green dress. But this time she had a face. My mother said she started to get scared, and then felt an overwhelming sense of warmth. When my mother started to walk toward the vision, it went up the stairway and disappeared.

"Later that night, my sister was sleeping with me in my bedroom and we both saw her, the Lady in Green. But we weren't afraid."

Apparently, Susan wasn't the only kid on the block to experience the bizarre.

"It wasn't just in our house," Susan said. "A boy who lived three doors down the street told us, without us saying anything about the Lady in Green, that there was a strange lady in his house. Maybe it was all over the neighborhood and nobody wanted to talk about it. I'm not saying we were built on a burial ground or anything like that, but there seemed to be something odd there, and I think it might have to do with being on the estate."

The furniture, that her father had sent home, seemed to have a life of its own after it arrived at the Beechfield Avenue home, Susan said.

"My father said he got it from the Old Sea Captain's son. He never explained any more than that. It was just the Old Sea Captain's furniture. It could have been bought for cheap or given as payment for an old debt."

There were several pieces, including a highboy dresser, a lower dresser, a woman's vanity, a stool and several removable mirrors that were affixed to the tops of both dressers and on the vanity. There were spokes, or pointed pieces of wood, protruding from the top of the furniture, where the mirrors could be screwed on.

The wood was dark mahogany, and there were lots of brass decorations and handles. All of the drawers locked with an old-fashioned, skeleton-type key.

There was no fancy carving of the wood, but anyone could tell the set was old and had been knocked around a bit.

The incident occurred about 15 years ago, around 1980. Susan's first husband was overseas, in the Army, and the young wife had gone home to live with her parents until his tour of duty was finished.

"It was time to go to bed," Susan recalled. "I was sleeping with my Mom in a large, queen-size bed. I had just started to doze off. You know, that period of time when you're just about to fall asleep, but you can see what's happening around you, but you can't move because you're so weak and almost out of it.

"I remember looking at the dresser, and I saw a face.

"It was staring at me, coming out from behind the dark brown, mahogany swirls. When I realized what I was seeing, I shook my head, to see if I was dreaming, but it was still there."

Susan paused a minute to remember the incident.

The room was dark, she said. It was late evening. But the face glowed. That's why she could remember it so clearly. It also seemed to be coming out from the closed drawer near the top of the highboy, the one next to the top level. But the drawer wasn't open, and the face seemed to be floating out from the wood.

> "It was staring at me, coming out from behind the dark brown, mahogany swirls."

"It was an old face," she said. "As old faces go, it was not scary, not a horror movie type. And I remember it had lots of hair, even though it was old. Long, dark black hair that was shoulder length. Like the style a pirate would wear.

"When I realized what was happening, I curled up like a ball, trying to get out of its way. 'Cause it was coming right toward me, and I could hear it whispering."

Sensing Susan's movement in the bed, her mother woke up and saw it.

"As soon as Mom saw it, she let out a scream," Susan said, "and the face, it went right back into the wood. I can still see my mother holding me and telling me everything is going to be okay."

Susan and her mother went downstairs and sat up talking for the rest of the night. The next morning they moved the Sea Captain's dresser to the corner of the room farthest from the bed, but that was the last time they ever saw anything crawl out from that particular piece of furniture.

"It wasn't too much longer after that when Mom sold the whole set to an antique dealer," Susan said. "But she kept one of the mirrors, and then another strange thing happened."

Susan said her mother would prop up the mirror, which was about two feet high, against the wall on top of a low dresser, so she could use it when she got dressed. She liked it because it was the perfect size for what she needed.

A picture of Susan's grandmother that had always been standing on the center of the dresser top began moving to the farthest end and turning to face a different direction whenever Susan's mother left the Sea Captain's mirror on the top of the dresser.

"Grandmother's picture kept moving away, as if it didn't want to be near the mirror. It was crazy, and I saw it happen, and more than once."

One can't be sure if it was the furniture or the house that may have caused the strange events that Susan witnessed. She talked about the old woman, with the bony fingers, who tried to strangle her first husband while he slept, and the force that pushed him up against the shower walls in the second-floor bathroom.

"He left for good the night he woke up and found 10 people—or spirits or ghosts or whatever you want to call them—standing all around his bed, talking like they were at a party. He stayed up all night, downstairs, and left for good after that. It didn't matter that much," Susan added, "we were pretty much on the outs anyway, but after that he couldn't take it anymore."

Things have been pretty calm for Susan during the last few years. She's remarried, moved into a newer home in

Catonsville and even was able to stop psychic things from starting up again.

"A psychologist told me, 'Look, if things get started, as soon as they begin, you tell them to get out! They won't stay if you don't want them there.'

"My second husband doesn't want anything strange to happen, especially after hearing what happened before. When something squeezed my shoulder in this new house we're in, I said, 'I really don't need anything like this around anymore. So leave me alone.' And they did.

"But," Susan said—in a tone almost longing for some of the excitement of the past, or maybe it was just to find an answer to the hanging questions—"I'd really like to go up to my old house and ask the people who live there now if anything has ever happened to them. You never know if the Lady in Green or the Sea Captain are still around. Sometimes I just think back to those incidents, and you know, you just can't help wondering if they're still there."

The Invisible Lamplighter

avid King admitted that he couldn't resist a bargain, even if he didn't like the particular item that he had discovered.

In this unusual case, the object of his attention was a 1950s Fenton, poppy lamp. Since David collected pottery and glassware, especially Fenton, he said he should have been more excited about his find. But the lamp was lime green, not a color he liked—nor was it easy to match with other pieces or standard decor.

Nevertheless, David—23 years old and the owner of several small businesses in Walhalla, South Carolina—purchased the lamp and took it home.

"My mother was sick at the time, and she was recuperating in a hospital bed that I had set up in the living room," he recalled. "I put the lamp on one of the tables, out of her immediate reach, across the room from the bed."

David described the piece as a two-section lamp, with one globe atop the other and a thinner, center section in between. It was electric, with a brass switch in the base. Despite its color, the glasswork was attractive, with ruffles on the top part of the glass.

That first night, neither David nor his mother paid much attention to the lamp. They remember thinking that the lamp, which had been on, had somehow turned itself off in the middle of the night. But they didn't give it any further thought.

The second night after the lamp's arrival, David's mother was awakened by a light in the room. She gathered her thoughts and focused on the lamp's glow, then began to try to get out of bed to turn it off. But the lamp went dark on its own, and she fell back to sleep.

"The third night it happened," David said, "we became very suspicious. We noticed that it seemed to light up about the same time. After that we took to watching the lamp. In fact, we sat up, in the dark, waiting for it to turn on."

They weren't disappointed.

Each night, exactly at one in the morning, the unique lamp turned on with a definite "click," and that same sound was repeated one minute later as the distinctive "click" signaled the switch shutting off.

"We mentioned it to a few friends, but they thought we were crazy," David said, laughing lightly at the memory.

Eventually, a select list of close friends became believers.

"Our next door neighbors came over, and the light came on for them, just like it did for us. After a few more nights, we unplugged it and put it in a box. But," David said, "we'd eventually pull it out again and set it up. And it would do the same thing—turn on at one o'clock, sharp."

> "OUR NEXT DOOR NEIGHBORS CAME OVER, AND THE LIGHT CAME ON FOR THEM, JUST LIKE IT DID FOR US."

Concerned that it might be some problem with the lamp's electrical cord or the wiring in that section of his house, David tried the lamp in several different outlets in various rooms. In each case, the light came on at the very same time every morning when it was plugged in.

"To check it out further, I took it over to a friend's house. He had seen it light up in my house, so he was aware of what was going on. We made sure it was shut off, and we plugged it in there," David said. "We were sitting in front of his TV, eating popcorn and watching some videos. In fact, we had forgotten about the lamp. But at one o'clock it turned on, in his house.

"We laughed at first, because we weren't really expecting it to turn on in his house. Well, I was, but he wasn't, even though he'd seen it happen in my house. I remember, he said, 'So you brought it over here with the ghost, so you can take it back and make sure the ghost goes with you.'"

David admitted that he sometimes feels a little uneasy, but it is a very nicely etched lamp, with a distinctive design, even though he still doesn't care for the color.

One interesting aspect of the puzzle, David pointed out, is that his lamp somehow follows the time on the clock in the house where it is plugged in. It does not react according to wristwatch time or any other personal timepiece.

"We found that it stays on for exactly one minute," David said. "We've timed it and looked at the clock. When the clock's hand hits the 1, it turns on with its own power.

"It really makes your hair stand on end sometimes, when you hear that distinctive 'click' when it goes on and off. It's just so eerie."

David made a trip back to the auction house where he had bought the lamp and inquired about its origin. He was told that the piece had come from an estate in Greenville, South Carolina. The owner had died in the middle of the night and was found, alone in his bed, the following morning.

One of David's friends suggested that the original owner had turned the light on at exactly one o'clock, and he may have been trying to get to his pills when he died one minute later.

"I don't have any better reason for what happens," David said, "and I don't try to figure it out. I just accept the fact that it turns on at the same time every night."

The lime green Fenton lamp still rests on the table where David placed it that first day he brought it home.

"We've taken it off there a few times and packed it away. But, after a few days, we seem to always bring it back. It doesn't go on when it's unplugged."

David admitted it was the "great deal" that caused him to purchase the lamp. "It matches absolutely nothing else in my house. I'll probably keep it because it's entertaining, at least in a morbid sort of way. But, like I tell my friends," David said, with a hint of laughter in his voice, "the fact is, we've got a haunted lamp. That's the only logical explanation I can come up with."

Author's Note: David King mentioned that he and a few friends gathered near the Fenton lamp and read aloud the advance copy of this story. Since the reading that night, the lamp has not turned on under its own power.

"I think that was very eerie," David said. "In fact, I think that bothered me more than anything else."

Haunted Headboard

*N*ow in her early 40s, Ann can still remember the summer of 1969, when she was 15 years old and her family lived in a second-floor apartment in Arbutus, southwest of Baltimore, Maryland.

"I was a happy kid," she said. "I had a wonderful life. Things were really pretty normal."

She can recall the incidents during that Saturday afternoon, when her mother and father were unloading her surprise from the pickup truck they had borrowed from a friend.

"I ran out into the parking lot, I was so excited," she said. "They were bringing in a new bedroom set, just for me. It wasn't a hand-me-down, but brand new. It was beautiful, smooth dark wood, and there was a tall dresser, plus a lower one with a wide mirror that sat on it and a smooth polished headboard for my bed."

A few days after Ann's bedroom had been rearranged, she was alone, resting happily in her new bed late at night.

"I heard a steady tapping. It was like a steady, even-sounding tap . . . tap . . . tap . . . " Ann recalled. "It went on for a long time, a good 15 minutes without stopping."

She remembered trying to figure out both the cause and the source of the odd, repetitive sounds.

"I thought, maybe the sound was from my moving or breathing, and that maybe something was loose. I figured my headboard had not been screwed tight enough," Ann explained. "I tried not to breath, keep real still.

"When it didn't stop, I got up, turned on the light and looked under the bed. There was nothing. But the sound was still there. It was so loud, I could hear it standing next to the light switch across the room."

For the next hour, Ann knelt on her mattress at the foot of her bed, staring at the dark headboard. She awoke the next morning and discovered she was curled up on the rug, on the floor, beside the bottom end of her bed.

"The next day, the tapping became more frantic and louder," Ann said. "It wasn't a steady tapping any more," she said, explaining that there were groups of sounds, coming in long and short sequences, and in different series of twos and threes.

"It was like Morse code. I didn't understand it. But I remember thinking it was like someone was trying to tell me something. I didn't understand Morse code, and, to tell you the truth, I'm glad I didn't."

The second night, surrounded by her new bedroom set, Ann slept on the floor, huddled up in the far corner of her room. Like the night before, she had fallen asleep outside of her bed.

The next day, Ann had her father check the headboard screws at the base of her bed. They were fine, he said, and he feared he would strip the screws if he tried to make them any tighter. She had told her parents about the tapping, but they said it was her "overworked imagination."

That night, when the noise started, it was so loud she couldn't concentrate.

Ann used her bedroom phone and called Sandy, her best friend. The confused girl held the receiver of her phone near the headboard and asked Sandy to describe what she was hearing.

Ann recalled the conversation. "She said, 'It sounds like someone's tapping.' I said, 'Yeah! It's my headboard.' Then Sandy said, 'No way! You're doing that yourself.'"

Thinking back more than 25 years, Ann said she clearly remembers that the sound was like a long fingernail striking against solid wood. It's the only way she could duplicate the sound.

"By now it was getting louder, very loud," she said. "To me it was erratic, frantic, as if someone or something was very frustrated. It got to the point where it was getting on my nerves, but I was never afraid."

Ann said the annoying tapping would continue all night long. She felt that, whatever it was, it seemed to be trying to wake her up, so she couldn't get any rest. After about a month, she shared the situation with her 21-year-old brother, Danny.

"That's when I really started to freak out," Ann said. "He suggested I might have a ghost trapped in the headboard. I told him that was impossible, especially since the furniture was brand new.

"Maybe the driver went through the windshield and smashed his head against the trunk, and his blood is inside the wood in your headboard."

"That's when he smiled at me, like he knew it all, and said, with an evil grin, 'How do you know it wasn't built from an old tree that somebody was hung from, or maybe the wood came from a tree that was hit by a car in an accident. Maybe the driver went through the windshield and smashed his head against the trunk, and his blood is inside the wood in your headboard.'

"I never thought about anything spooky until he said that, then it started bothering me. Being 15 and an impressionable teenager, you go see spooky movies and come home shaking. And here I was with a strange thing in my own house, right in my very own room. I didn't want to hear anything else from Danny."

Ann said she would sit at the foot of her bed and stare at the smooth, dark headboard, with its plain front and small spindles, and just wonder . . . for over an hour at a time, getting almost hypnotized by the continuous tapping.

"I wondered what if someone is in there trying to talk to me. I got the feeling that, whatever it was, it was getting real frantic and desperate. The sound was speeding up and going crazy. I couldn't take it anymore. I got a pair of pliers, crawled underneath the bed and took the headboard off."

Hoping for the best, she placed the headboard under her double bed, flat and unused.

But the sound of the tapping continued to reach her ears from underneath her mattress. It was loud enough so that she still couldn't sleep.

"One day, I carried it downstairs and put it in the basement storage room," Ann said, "I didn't hear it. But, whenever I went down there to get anything, and was there long enough, I could hear it. I finally decided it was time for the headboard to move on."

Although her parents were upset with her decision, Ann said they finally realized she wouldn't use it. They also didn't want to take up storage space with something that would never be used.

Ann offered the piece of restless furniture to her best friend's mother. Even though Sandy's mother admitted that she had heard about the tapping, she agreed to accept the headboard.

"At first it didn't bother her, but as time went on, Sandy told me her mother got tired of the noises, too," Ann said.

The new owners lived in an old, Baltimore city row house. They eventually disconnected the headboard and left it out in the hallway, resting against the wall between the door to Sandy's bedroom and the one to her mother's room, that was further down the hall.

Sandy, who like Ann was 15 years old at the time, awoke suddenly one dark morning. She had been disturbed by an unusual creaking sound in her bedroom.

Sitting upright in bed, the teenager saw a young, blond-headed boy and screamed. He was dressed in khaki pants and a plaid shirt. She saw the figure float rapidly out of the room, through the wall, and onto the upstairs hallway.

By the time Sandy got out of bed and raced to the hall, her mother, who had heard the scream, opened her door from the adjoining room. The two women faced each other in the second floor hall, just in time to see the boy—in khaki pants and colorful shirt—jump into the headboard and disappear.

Recalling the incident, Ann's tone suddenly turned soft and serious, "Sandy told me her mother looked at her startled face and said, 'I saw him, too.' They got rid of the headboard soon after that night. I have no idea who it went to—the Salvation Army, I think. And who knows where it is now? That was over 25 years ago.

"Sometimes, thinking back, I wish I knew what it was or what he was saying, trying to tell me. The tapping was so frantic, so impatient, at times. It was like it was desperate to talk to someone, like it wanted to tell its story.

"I guess now we'll never know."

The Jade Ring

olly and Kevin had been together a long time. They had met in the sixth grade, started dating just before their senior year of high school and got married while they were still in college.

Neither of them had gone out with anyone else. It was just the two of them.

Unfortunately, the marriage didn't last. Within six months it was over. But, Holly said, they never stopped caring for each other, and they continued to have a unique bond, a "special gift" is how Holly explained it.

"We always had a very good rapport, and we each seemed to know what the other person was thinking," said Holly. Now 45, she pleasantly recalled the interesting incidents that had occurred nearly 30 years ago.

"We experienced a lot of coincidences, like going to the store, or the library or the shopping mall, and finding the other person there. We laughed a lot about it, teased each other that maybe we were checking up on each other.

"The strangest thing," Holly added, "is when I'd go to dial his number. I'd just pick up the phone—it didn't even have a chance to ring—and he'd be there on the line. Or I'd be thinking of calling him and the phone would ring and it would be Kevin.

"I'm not talking a few times a year, it happened several times a month. It even continued to occur during the years following our divorce."

Holly said Kevin had precognitive dreams. She said he often would describe something that was going to happen. At times, he even knew the topic of an upcoming conversation and would tell her portions of the dialog.

"One time," Holly recalled, "we were driving through an unfamiliar section of Cincinnati. On this occasion, he never described the outside of the building, but when we arrived there I knew it was the place he had talked about after having one of his dreams. From the moment I passed over the threshold of this old messy junk store, I knew this was the place. He even had imitated the accent of the shopkeeper, when he had described the dream to me earlier. When we were there, we found the Pink Willow plate he told me we could find. He had described it all from his dream.

"It would frighten him, but it wouldn't bother me. They were very intense deja vu experiences—vivid and descriptive enough to make the results recognizable to me or his mother when he told us about them."

Although the marriage didn't work out, Kevin and Holly kept in touch. Years after the divorce, in 1989, she got a call from Kevin's mother telling her that he had been involved in an automobile accident. He was in the hospital for about a week before he died. Because of his appearance, his mother decided to have him cremated.

For the next year, Kevin's ashes were in a sealed container the size of a hardbound book. The heavy, but compact, repository of his ashes was passed among his mother, grandmother and former wife.

"We sort of had joint custody," Holly said, smiling. "We hadn't planned on it, but it just occurred. On my 40th birthday, I borrowed the ashes for old times' sake. Kevin and I sat and watched the *Batman* video together. He really liked those sort of adventure movies, so I thought it would be nice if he saw the show. We spent the evening together. I recalled how he used to tease me and say I would be over the hill at 40. He didn't make it that far, and I did."

Holly said Kevin's grandmother didn't get a chance to see him in the hospital before he died, so his ashes were with her for a period of time.

"It was okay with her," Holly said. "She said she felt okay having him around, and it didn't bother me either. I sort of liked having him with me."

When they were dating, Holly said she and Kevin would talk about the possibilities of eternity and the hereafter. They had different opinions of what would occur after death.

She believed in some form of reincarnation or a continuing process of being. But Kevin used to say: "When you're dead, you're dead, and that's the end of it." To him, there was nothing at the other end.

But, Holly recalled, no matter what he believed, he still told his mother that if there was a way to get in contact with her after he was gone he would do so.

He never did.

Instead, he got in touch with his former wife, twice.

Two years after Kevin's funeral, while Holly was outside her new home, hammering some nails to fix a loose board on a fence, she heard a voice . . . Kevin's voice.

"I heard him say, 'Holly. Sometimes you can be such a tomboy!' When I heard it, I stopped and looked around. I didn't believe it. It was right up against my ear, so real that I jumped. I was startled. It was really strange. I remember getting goose bumps, and I know it wasn't my imagination. I heard it, heard him."

The other unusual incident, however, was his contact through a ring, a jade ring.

After they had become engaged, Kevin bought himself a solid, dark green, jade ring that was backed with a thick gold band. He wore it for three years on his little finger. It became Holly's wedding ring when they were married.

"I wore it for a while, even after we were divorced," said Holly, "but, eventually, I gained some weight and it didn't fit any more. So I put it in a velvet-lined box in my safe-deposit box."

"I opened the jewelry box," Holly said, *"and the first thing I saw was the crack."*

A day or two after Kevin's accident, while he was still in the hospital, Holly went to the bank to use her safe-deposit box. She opened the container holding the jade ring. For some reason, she took it out and looked it over, held it tightly and placed it back into the tight cushion in the small ring box.

One week after Kevin died and was cremated, she returned to the box to get the ring. She thought it might be good to put it in the small niche of the memorial wall where his ashes, eventually, were going to be placed.

"I opened the jewelry box," Holly said, "and the first

thing I saw was the crack. The jade band was cracked completely, from the top edge of the ring to the bottom, and all the way through. The space was so wide, you could see the gold of the band underneath.

"How could it happen? It was in a safe-deposit box. It wasn't going anywhere. It didn't drop. There wasn't any temperature change. It was locked up and no one except me could get to it.

"I was amazed. I thought of it as a special signal. I just knew it had to represent a final separation between us."

Holly explained that even though she and Kevin were divorced, they were still a part of each other's lives. They could rely upon each other. They had been good friends, very special friends.

"The only people I ever told this story to are his mother and my husband," said Holly. "His mother believed, without a doubt, it was a definite sign. But she's still waiting for him to contact her directly, rather than through me.

"But I still keep in touch with her. We're good friends, and we were brought together through Kevin. I'm satisfied he's at rest now. When his ashes were placed into the memorial wall at Spring Grove Cemetery, I put the ring, our jade ring, in his niche."

Unframed in Maine

*I*t started by chance, as most unusual things happen, early in the spring of 1992. Sally Hoffman was at a public sale in Skowhegan, Maine, about a one-hour drive west of Bangor. She felt good about being out and about after experiencing months of cabin fever.

She stood in the midst of the audience, interested in the picture the auctioneer was holding.

She bid . . . higher . . . higher . . . .

Just high enough.

Sally had signaled for the top price and the lot was hers—both pieces.

"I bought the two pieces because they came in a lot," she said, recalling the day very clearly. "I knew I didn't want the second print. Well, I thought the picture in the frame was a print. But I felt I could sell that frame even if I didn't like the picture."

Sally said the unwanted picture's image was a black-and-white, sepia type image, with a pastel, chalk-colored look. The 1920s era portrait, she said, offered an "unusual and rather interesting" appearance. Actually, the picture seemed to present, or contain, two images, depending upon how one looked at it.

"The picture was that of a woman, wearing a long, dark, full-length coat," Sally said. "It was a vertical image. She seemed to be holding a handkerchief. But, if you looked at it sometimes, you would see a different image. You could see a woman in a dress. And, instead of a handkerchief, she was holding a small bouquet of flowers."

Sally kept the photograph in her office, located in a room in the downstairs of her home. There was a hallway—with closets that housed the air conditioning unit and heater—

between her office and the door that led into the basement-level garage.

On April 1st, Sally recalled removing the frame from the picture. It was quite nice, wooden, and she sold it almost immediately.

She propped the unframed photograph up against the front of a couch in her office, with the base resting on the seat cushions. For almost a week it sat there, the woman's face staring across the room at Sally as she worked at her desk.

Sally thought all the mechanical systems in her home were in good condition. She had never experienced problems in the past. But, for some unknown reason, a huge puff of smoke shot out of her oil burner, located in a basement closet adjacent to her office.

After fixing the furnace, the repairman said he could discover no logical reason for the breakdown.

A few days later, activity began to pick up. On April 7, the date of her wedding anniversary, Sally was talking long distance to her husband who works in New York.

"I'm upstairs, in the kitchen, talking on the phone, and the fax machine starts up and is printing blank sheets of paper in the office. I have an extra long cord on the phone, so I walked downstairs and could see it happening while I was talking to my husband. But," Sally added, "I hadn't turned it on, and, it can only work when I'm not using the phone."

Sally told her husband that the fax was working on its own. They laughingly said it was celebrating its birthday, since they had gotten it for their anniversary the year before. Eventually, the machine stopped. There was no message on the blank sheets of paper it had distributed in the downstairs office.

"Next," Sally said, "the answering machine went on the fritz, and the phone stopped working. I sent them both out to be fixed."

On April 15th, as she was finishing up her income taxes (it was the first time she had waited that long, she said), her computer would not accept her disks that contained her tax information.

"I had to get extension forms and file later," Sally recalled, frustration rising in her voice as she recalled the series of events. She sent the computer out for repair and received a new set of tax form disks that she had to use. But, several months later, when she tried to install the files from the new disks, she found that the original files—that she had tried to install in the computer in April—were already on the machine.

In late April, Sally was discussing the antique business with a friend who asked her if she ever thought she had brought any spirits into her home with the items she found.

Sally said, "I told her, 'I never did before, but I think so now.'"

Sitting at her desk, Sally looked at the photograph, that was still resting on the couch. She then looked counterclockwise, from right to left. It was then she noticed that each item of equipment in her home that had broken down, since April 1st when she removed the frame, was affected in a logical pattern moving from right to left.

The oil burner in the hall. Then the fax machine near the couch. Then the answering machine and telephone. Next the computer.

"It was as if someone was systematically going around the room and working their way, in a counterclockwise motion, investigating things that they had never seen before.

"I looked at the picture and felt that the woman, who had been trapped behind the glass and in the frame, had been let out and was encountering a whole world that she hadn't experienced. I actually got the feeling that she had been walking around the room, like someone who was picking these things up and shaking them to see how they worked.

"That's when I got the idea that all of this was coming from the picture of the woman on the couch. But I wasn't afraid of her."

Sally admitted that she began talking to the picture, telling her she understood that she might be curious, that these things she was toying with weren't around in the 1920s.

"But I also told her I couldn't allow her to continue doing this exploration, because it was costing me a fortune."

One of the most unusual events associated with the photograph took place the day a repairman noticed the picture in Sally's office. She said he became very upset and asked her if she was going to keep the photograph. He gave her the impression that she was crazy for having it, but he would not offer any explanation as to why. He was the husband of an acquaintance, and he left the home very quickly after arriving.

To this day, she said, she has not been able to obtain an explanation or reason for his extremely uncomfortable reaction to the picture.

The last mechanical malfunction occurred to her copy machine. Sally entered her office one morning to discover black toner flying into the air.

"It was going all over the place, in puffs," Sally said. "It was pouring out. The machine was just sitting there, and it was turned off. But toner was coming out of the flip cover, pouring out of the bottom, getting all over my silver gray carpet.

"I knew it was her! I said 'This is it!' I couldn't keep the picture after that.

"The sad thing was, I wanted to investigate it," she added. "I wanted to find out the answers to a lot of questions:

Did I really have a ghost?

Was there a person here who had been let out of the frame?

Who was this person who had been imprisoned behind the glass?

Where did she come from?

Was it someone that I knew?

What was she trying to tell me?

Was all of this an effort to attract my attention?

Was she unhappy with having had her picture taken?"

"Did I really have a ghost? Was there a person here who had been let out of the frame? Who was this person who had been imprisoned behind the glass?"

Sally admitted she was extremely frustrated. It was obvious she could not afford to let the restless spirit continue to roam her home. Up to that point, the happy wanderer had limited her explorations to the basement.

Upstairs there were larger, more interesting and more expensive toys to destroy—including the washer and dryer, refrigerator, stove, dishwasher, television, VCR . . . . The potential for serious damage was substantial, and the level of the mysterious guest's curiosity seemed to be quite high.

Sally said there was no one, except her husband, with whom she could discuss the matter, and she saw no quick solution in sight.

"This was not the kind of thing you go telling people," she said. "They think you're a lunatic."

Sally solved her association with the photograph by taking it to an antique cooperative and placing it up for sale.

During that brief interim period that the photograph lived at the shop, the manager—who was unaware of any of the strange incidents that occurred at Sally's home—said in the mornings he found the shop doors unlocked, the lights turned on, items knocked over and jewelry taken out of cabinets and strewn around the floor.

"The next thing I knew it was gone, sold," Sally said. "We don't know where she's gone and what else she has done. And I've not had any problems since."

Reflecting on her unusual experiences, Sally said, "Something strange happened in this house. It happened while this picture was here. I don't need proof. I know!

"I know there was a woman here. She had been let out of that frame and she was curious. But I was never afraid and I didn't have any feeling that this person wanted to hurt me in any way, even while she was wrecking my house. In the end, I just couldn't afford to keep her here."

The Old Hotel Washstand

larington, Pennsylvania, is in the northwest corner of the state, in the mountains of Forest County.

Back in the late 1800s—when loggers would ship cut timber by way of the Clarion River to Pittsburgh—the area's population was up to 5,000 and there were large hotels, fancy gaming saloons, big boarding houses, blacksmith shops, just about everything a city would need.

More than that, it even had its own baseball team.

Today, the village has only a handful of registered voters, less than a hundred, and you can hardly find any traces left of the original town. Most of the land is used by retirees, campers and hunters.

Roger and Mary Hare of Hampstead, North Carolina, know about Clarington. They lived up there for a number of years after they retired. They have been married for 40 years and have been collecting antiques for at least that long. For a short while they were dealers, but they're out of the business now. They still enjoy looking at their antique furniture and recalling the interesting stories associated with each find.

Roger described the visit he and Mary made to an old homestead farm, out near Zimmerman Hill, not too far from Clarington, back in 1988, when all of the contents were being sold off.

"I went by an old washstand that was just setting there in the bedroom," said Roger. "It had no mirror or rack, and it was painted pink and blue. Then we went out into the chicken coop, and there was another part of that washstand."

"We recognized it, because it was painted pink and blue, too," Mary said. "Then we went out into the barn and found the mirror. All three pieces were painted pink and blue."

Roger said they took the washstand back to their house in New Castle, where they lived at the time. They stripped it down, refinished it and brought it back to its original condition, except for a small circle on the left-hand top that had been burned by oil spilled from a burning lamp.

The couple described the piece as a solid oak cabinet, with one right-handed door that opened in the front of the base, two drawers on the left and a longer drawer that went across the top front.

The base was solid wood and a bowl of water could be placed in the center. On one side the mirror was attached and the towel rack extended up on the opposite side.

After they completed their revival of the wooden piece, Roger and Mary decided to take it up to their cabin outside Clarington.

Even though the piece would not match the Victorian furniture in their cabin's bedroom, they were proud of the finished product and decided to place it in the room.

"From the minute we got the washstand up there, it started," Mary said, referring to the series of unusual events that had taken place.

"Every night, at 4 a.m., after we moved in with the washstand, it sounded like laughing and yelling at a party. It was like a crowd of people laughing and talking," Roger said.

Mary was the first person to hear the noise, and she woke her husband and told him there was a party going on outside.

"I looked at her and said, 'There's nobody around here having a party at four o'clock in the morning.' I got up and looked out, and the woods were pitch black, and we were living out deep in the woods."

The couple explained that the sound would last about 20 minutes every night of the week, and it continued to occur regularly . . . not for a week, nor a month, but for a very long time. The 4 a.m. party wake-up call occurred each night for the four years the Hares lived in Clarington.

"It was like a huge batch of people in a hotel, barroom or dance hall," Roger said. "Like they were having a ball, like there was a big party."

"You could hear bottles hitting the tables and glasses tapping," said Mary. "Big, gruff men were talking, and women were laughing."

As the years passed, Roger and Mary admitted that they just got used to it and laughed it off as an unexplained event.

"We couldn't figure it out," she said, "so we decided we had to live with it. We also never told anyone about what was happening."

After Roger Junior was married, his parents invited him and his new bride to spend some time at the cabin. Since it was sort of a honeymoon event, the Hares offered their Victorian bedroom to their son and his new wife.

"Every night, at 4 a.m., it sounded like laughing and yelling at a party. It was like a crowd of people laughing and talking."

The morning after his first night sleeping in the Victorian room, Roger Junior arrived at breakfast and asked, with all seriousness, "Why didn't you tell me if you were going to have a party at four in the morning? I could hear the goings on for a while and then I fell back asleep."

His parents told him about what they had been hearing each night, and the young man confirmed that it also had happened to him.

"He said he heard it plain as day," said Mary. "In fact, he was a little bit upset with us for not calling him downstairs to what he thought was our party."

The Hares discussed the situation on several occasions and wondered if their house was haunted or if the cabin had been built on an old Indian burial ground.

While visiting the cabin, an antique dealer, who was a friend of Roger's, noticed the old washstand and said it would fit in perfectly with several other pieces he had.

They reached an agreement, and the piece was taken away to New Jersey, where it was sold immediately to a visitor to the shop.

"As soon as it left," Mary said, "I didn't hear the noise anymore."

Her husband agreed, "When that old washstand left, we never heard anything like those sounds again. But," he added, "you'd expect it to happen, like it always did."

"It was so quiet," Mary said, "I couldn't sleep. I had gotten to the point of waiting for the party to start. I think about it a lot. It was just like a barroom on a Saturday night, when everybody was celebrating. Like a lot of talking an' jabberin'."

"It was just happy times, happy sounds," Roger added.

Roger still talks about the stories of the days when they rafted all that timber down the Clarion River, and the boom times and the action in the mountain town.

"The fella that bought the washstand from us," said Roger, "he told us it came out of an old hotel. That's why he called it a hotel washstand. I believe it probably was taken out of one of the old hotels and sold, after the town went downhill. Then, it was just sitting in that old farmhouse, all separated apart and painted over, waiting to be brought back.

"After we refinished it and brought it back up to the cabin, near to the town where it was before, things just all came back, the good times, the sounds of the people during the town's good old days."

"Maybe," added Mary, "strange things were happening in that old farmhouse, where we found it, and that's why they had separated it in pieces."

"We haven't told this story to too many people," admitted Roger. "Some of them give you sort of a strange look. Then the others, they wonder about the story, but they know we couldn't come up with something like this on our own."

Portal in the Glass

he painting caught Debbie Keri-Brown's eye. *The dark, narrow frame doesn't do the artwork justice,* Debbie thought, but something caused her to pause, drew her closer to examine this one piece, select it from among the several thousand items that were squeezed into every corner and niche of the suburban antique mall.

From her home in Ohio, the dealer estimated that the artwork was painted in the 1920s or '30s. It was a moderate size, about 20 inches wide and 14 inches high.

To her, the painting is still special and, after eight years, it still hangs in a prominent spot in her home.

"It's a beautiful painting of four young girls, who are about 10 to 14 years old," Debbie said. "They are wearing pastel-colored, flowered, ankle-length dresses. They're holding hands and dancing in a circle. One interesting thing is that the background is very faint, and is painted in a way that you can't really tell if they are inside or outdoors."

Debbie said the painting presents an "angelic" impression and a sense of calmness. While the work is quite detailed, the entire piece has a cloudlike quality that seems muted and flowing.

"There's something about it that makes me feel that they are angels dancing up in heaven," Debbie added. "Maybe it's the impression of innocence that made me immediately fall in love with it. But, I can still remember that frame was not attractive."

The first thing Debbie planned to do with her new find was replace the frame with another that she had purchased the same day for that specific purpose.

When she arrived home, she took the glass from the second frame and left it out in the garage. She also sent her angelic painting to an art shop to be cleaned and rematted.

A few days later, when she arrived home with the newly matted work, Debbie stepped on the glass that she had stored in the garage. She said she was bothered by the accident, but immediately purchased another piece of glass.

When she came home with the replacement glass, Debbie felt it slip from her grasp and watched it smash into hundreds of pieces.

"I'm an antique dealer," she said, sharing the frustration she felt at the time. "I'm very careful, and now I had to go out and buy a third glass for this painting. When I got that glass home, I was very careful, handling it gently as I placed it in the frame that was going to hold the picture of the four girls.

"As I placed the last corner of the glass in the frame, and positioned it to lay firmly in place, a small crack developed, and expanded, in the top, left-hand corner."

Debbie said the thin line gradually moved across the glass from a spot—about two inches below the upper left corner—and travelled diagonally toward the top of the frame.

"It formed a rough triangle. It never shattered, it was a very clean crack. I was amazed," Debbie said. "After replacing the glass three times, I figured the angelic beings in the picture didn't want glass on top of them, or maybe they wanted air or some small means to escape."

Debbie never bothered to get that third piece of glass replaced, just sealed up the back of the painting and hung the artwork in her family room.

"My feeling was that they don't want it changed, so I left it alone. The crack actually goes across the matting, so it doesn't affect the picture itself," she explained.

Debbie's unnamed, angelic painting still hangs, accented by the gold-leafed, antique frame that she bought for the piece. The straight, smooth sections, and the ornate corners with brass scrollwork, add dignity and grace to the artwork.

"It's just such a beautiful painting," she said. "The figures are so lifelike. When you look at them, you see and feel a sense of peace. Maybe the crack in the glass is a portal for them to use when coming and going."

46

Jonathan's Special Chair

onathan was excited about his trip. Even though the end of November was not the best time of the year to be traveling, and even if it was a long, lonely drive to Western Maryland, he had decided that the trip was definitely going to be worth it.

The Portland Cutter Sleigh that he was planning to buy was exactly what he had been seeking. He could tell from the picture he had received in the mail. There also were some other pieces that he was interested in securing for his store.

His sources were a few "pickers," people who aren't full-time dealers but who buy interesting things now and then and sell them on the side. Jonathan had found some unusual items using this avenue in the past.

He promised Victoria, his wife, that the old wooden antique sleigh would dress up the shop window for Christmas. Plus, when they sold it, the profit would be well worth the time and effort he had spent on the trip.

His destination was a small homestead past Cumberland, almost near the Pennsylvania-West Virginia border.

He stopped several times along the route, made what he considered to be a few smart deals and arrived at the old farmhouse to pick up the sleigh on schedule. He was delighted that he also was able to purchase a handsome hand-carved chair. Jonathan completed his business, loaded his van and attached U-Haul trailer and headed home.

He had been gone four days and arrived back at his antique shop, on the Western Shore of Maryland, in the middle of the morning. Immediately, he called a friend to help him unload.

The two men tried to get the sleigh into the store, but it wouldn't fit through the main door. They decided to store it elsewhere, but that meant it was not going to be the focus of the corner window Christmas display.

Instead, Jonathan filled the store window with the "special" chair. He and Victoria added some seasonal decorations, and they agreed it filled the space quite nicely.

After the holidays, the "unusual" chair remained a major item of the store's inventory. It had arrived at the end of November and sat for nearly three months in the window.

Jonathan recalled his reaction when he first saw the piece in the front room of the old Cumberland farmhouse.

"It immediately interested me," he said. "From my first touch, I found it was enchanting and troubling. To be honest," he added, "it scared the hell out of me. But I bought it because I was greedy about wanting something so intricately carved. It was ornate and grotesque at the same time."

He estimated that the chair had been made in Germany, about 1880, and was shipped to the U.S. from Berlin in 1903. The shipping tag was still attached to the underside of the seat.

It was large, thick and sturdy and a very dark, walnut color. Surprisingly, it was light in weight, like poplar wood, and not very dense.

It was assembled from two pieces, and easily dismantled and transportable. Perhaps its most striking features were the ornate carvings covering most of its surfaces.

The back of the chair featured the carved head of a gremlin, or a dwarf, that projected out about 2-1/2 inches from the flat surface.

There was a figure with the head of a bird—with the facial expression set in a wicked sneer—and it had a woman's breast and a man's ribs.

The top corner carvings featured the heads of flying dogs, and the feet were covered with fish heads, with snail like bodies and tails that turned into a spiders.

> "IT scared the hell out of me. But I bought it because I was greedy about wanting something so intricately carved. It was ornate and grotesque at the same time."

48

On the seat was a circle with a compass-like design.

"I didn't understand the significance of the chair," said Jonathan, reflecting back. "I was taken with it, attracted to it because it was so ornate, and I thought it would be good for the store, by attracting attention and customers. But I also was a bit wary, because it was so grotesquely carved, and I was overcome by its unusualness."

In February, Victoria had a contact from her friend in Louisiana. He was a psychic who had not been told anything about the chair.

"He called me," Victoria said. "He had visualized about the chair and he told me more about it than I could have told him. He was concerned about it being in the store. I remember his exact words, 'Get rid of it!' "

A bit bothered, Jonathan moved the chair out of the window and into the store, put a $1,400 price ticket on it and placed a number of books on top of it.

About mid-March, business picked up and people started coming in, frequently inquiring about the chair.

"There was one nice couple," Jonathan said. "I watched them as they approached the chair. They acted extremely careful, moved slowly, checking for faults and cracks all over. They handled the chair as if it was something sacred, reverently, the same way we might react if we had walked into a room and saw a crucifix and the other people didn't know what it was."

His curiosity aroused, Jonathan asked the examiners if they could share anything about the chair.

"They said they weren't quite sure, but they thought it might be a high priestess chair. They asked to move it to the center of the store. They went over it like it was an archaeological object."

Apparently, the people were seeking runes, the name for mystical symbols or markings that would help them determine the object's use. They said the carved face was probably "The Green Man," the God of Nature in German mythology. The winged figures at the top edges of the chair were protectors or guardians.

They pointed to the seat, that had a circular movable area that could be twisted or oriented in the direction of North, South, East and West, "to the four winds" they said.

"I was fascinated by the logic of their explanations," Jonathan said. "They explained that the chair was made of low density wood and able to be dismantled into two sections to make it more easily portable, so it could be carried from place to place.

"They told me they practiced white witchcraft, not casting evil spells but being one with nature and using the positive forces that nature could provide. They were from northern Pennsylvania, in their 40s and well-educated professionals. I got the impression that they were very interested in buying the chair. They also said that the seat was filled with some sort of energy field.

"Before they left, they pointed out other things associated with Wicca that I was ignorant of. In fact, they purchased a set of cufflinks that had been made in Salem, Massachusetts, and that bore the Wicca pentagram."

They never returned, but in April a man came in looking for books on witchcraft and noticed the chair. He went out to his car, came back in and asked if he could have a closer look.

With permission, he laid out five tarot cards on the seat and began to examine their significance.

"You have to understand," Jonathan said, "this was all brand new to a very conservative person. I was raised a Roman Catholic and had heard ghost stories, but I never experienced anything like this."

This man, too, began looking for runes. He explained that a person who practices white—the good and positive side of Wicca—witchcraft, wants nothing to do with the black side, and he didn't want to purchase an evil piece of furniture.

From the lack of certain markings and from the positive readings he received from his cards, the man determined the furniture was not dark or sinister.

More new people came into the store, many giving Jonathan information about his chair. Some told him the dog carvings on the top wings were guardians. Others said the scowling faces were meant to scare off intruders. The scratchings and rough marks symbolized defense.

"Soon afterwards, a young lady with a child came in and they moved directly to the chair," Jonathan said. "The mother put her arm over the seat of the chair, and the hair on her arm stood up on end. Now the chair was solid wood. There were no metal nails or pins in it. I went over and did it, too, and my hair stood up on end. It was right above the seated base. And it only happened sometimes, not always.

"I was starting to gain enough knowledge and see enough happening with the chair to be uncomfortable," Jonathan said.

About this time, Victoria had absorbed more than her fill of "the haunted chair," as she called it.

"I hated it!" she said without hesitation. "I didn't like it from the first day he brought it to the shop, because it was dark and demonic. Most of all, I was afraid he was going to bring it home."

"We also were concerned for our kids," Jonathan admitted. "We thought we could deal with whatever might happen, but we didn't want to put our children in harm's way. We also didn't want anyone who might be specifically interested in the chair coming to the house to see it. We wanted to keep our private life out of this whole situation."

Victoria got another telephone call from her psychic friend in Louisiana. When she told him what had occurred, he opened up and told her the piece of furniture was not to be feared as much as those persons it would bring to the store.

"He explained that the people coming," said Victoria, "were interested in using it for evil purposes, and because we happened to have it, we could be in a dangerous situation."

In an effort to sell the chair more quickly, Jonathan had put it back into the window. Suddenly things started happening in the store.

"We were having all sorts of new customers come in, constantly," Jonathan said, "but no one would buy a thing. Nothing at all. There were 80, 100 people in on a weekend. They would say, 'Oh, we just love your store' and then leave. We got lots of compliments. It was driving us crazy."

Another friend came by. She had not been in the store for months and, as she was leaving, Jonathan casually mentioned the high priestess chair in the window. She stopped dead and said she had a very bad feeling and she would consult some of her Wicca friends and get back with any information she could secure.

Within days, Jonathan got instructions to take the chair out of the window, immediately. His friend said the piece was a protectorate. It was specifically designed and built to protect its owner.

"Because it was not protecting anyone, because no one was sitting in the chair, it was protecting everything in the store," Jonathan said, "and not letting anything leave.

"I was told to take it out of the window and put it alone, in a corner, and give it a book to read, something nature related or some poetry, by placing it on the seat of the chair.

"To have some fun, I put a copy of Stephen King's *The Stand* on the chair's seat. But when my friend called and I told her what I had done, she ordered me to remove it immediately. She also sent me incense sticks to burn to cleanse the store.

"When we opened the next week, the first 10 people who came in bought something. We had people waiting in line to check out. Victoria and I were laughing we were so relieved."

The friend from Louisiana called and told Victoria the chair would be sold soon. But, he stressed that she and Jonathan must sell it only to the people who knew what the chair was to be used for, and that she and Jonathan were to receive some special sign before they made the deal.

Then he explained that the chair was a protector for travelers who used astral projection and expend energy to allow one's spirit to leave the body and go from one site to another.

However, the body is in a vulnerable state and subject to attack or injury during that time. The chair, with its energy and threatening carvings, protects the human body that has been left behind until the spirit force returns.

"The chair's purpose," said Jonathan, "was to protect the person who sat there while the spirit was traveling. That's also why it was important that it could be broken down and taken to different sites for gatherings and meetings."

In July, Victoria had a bothersome dream that the store was being ransacked. There were strange people, clad in white robes with greyhounds on leashes, shouting they were there to "Take out the light!" It was all so frightening and real. One red-headed woman, in particular, played a significant role in Victoria's dream.

That same day, Jonathan awoke later than usual and was late for work. When he arrived at the shop, there was a message from a friend that people were coming that evening, after hours, to see the chair.

Remembering that his Louisiana friend had said the buyers would come and would know what the chair is to used for, Jonathan arrived at 7 o'clock and began polishing the piece of furniture that had changed his life so dramatically.

At 7:15, two men and a woman walked through the door. But, for some reason, Jonathan did not get the impression that these were the people whom he was expecting.

They walked around the store, looking at nothing in particular.

"I remember the one man, he seemed very quiet, put his hands on the back of the chair," said Jonathan. "He said he was getting images. He said, 'I see a men's group in a tavern, like a Knights of Columbus or some fraternal organization, maybe Masons. They are gathered around. They know it is magical, but they don't know how to activate it.'

" 'I see a second family, years later, using the chair for petty things. They were trying to get their next door neighbor to sell them a cow, and they tried to influence others to do trivial things. These were far beneath the piece's level or capabilities. It's not what it was designed for. Later the chair sat idle for 40 years.'

"I asked the gentleman the purpose of the chair, and he told me he got the strong vision that it was a 'chariot used for traveling.' Finally, I was relieved, for I had someone who knew what it is for. No one else ever knew."

Jonathan asked the man if the chair could help with one's search for knowledge or spiritual growth.

The man answered, yes.

Then, as if enchanted with the possibilities of the powers associated with the chair, voices in the back of Jonathan's mind started telling him to keep the chair.

The man approached him and asked, "Are you going to sell it to us?"

Everything became dead quiet. Every sound ceased, the fans, electric current, all humming. It was as if a vacuum had sucked all the sound out of the air.

Jonathan replied without hesitation, "If I were going to sell it to anyone, it would be you, because I know you know what it's for. But I don't want to sell it."

As he completed the sentence, everything became dead quiet. Every sound ceased, the fans, electric current, all humming. It was as if a vacuum had sucked all the sound out of the air.

"I took that as a sign the chair wanted to go," Jonathan said. "I also was afraid that the chair, and its reaction to my desire to keep it, had put me in a dangerous situation.

"As I reflect on all of the strange things that happened during those months I'm amazed at how much I learned and about how much I still don't know. Things I had never imagined are now part of my life.

"I was the guardian of the chair, and I didn't want it stolen, damaged or destroyed. I also admit that I toyed with keeping it. But I didn't know how to deal with its powers. Perhaps those people did. If I didn't sell it to them, they probably could have gotten it somehow. They were powerful enough in their own way.

"I think the chair came to us to be protected for a period of time," said Jonathan, "and we were to bring the chair to where it could be found and eventually put to use. We were intermediaries. When I went out to buy the sleigh, I believe that it had enough energy to tell those people to sell it to me.

"So," Jonathan said, almost sadly, recalling the circumstances, "I made the sensible decision and told the man I would sell it to him."

Two days after their first visit, when the buyers came back into the store, Jonathan said they carried his chair away so very carefully.

"They almost treated it with reverence," he said. "In a way, I was relieved. But I also remember feeling like the light was going out, like the phrase the people were shouting in my wife's dream.

"Interestingly, there was another woman with them, who wasn't there the night they came in to buy the chair. She had bright red hair . . . just like in Victoria's dream.

"I never took a picture of the chair. I didn't have to, I will remember what it looks like forever. I also never inquired what they were going to do with the chair. I guess I really didn't want to know all the details at the time. Now, sometimes, I wonder who they were, how they found us and where they are now."

Jonathan said he has a better understanding of how pieces can be affected by the experiences of life, and he is more cautious now.

"Although the chair brought us great knowledge," he said, "We were out of our depth. While we learned a tremendous amount about that fantastic other world out there, we also were very vulnerable.

"Now that it's gone, I believe those people were meant to see it. It would draw certain people toward it. And you either liked it or hated it. Some people would walk past it, out in the open, and never know it existed. Others could find it if it was hidden behind stacks of books. It was almost like it was protecting itself and drawing energy off certain people who would pass."

Three weeks after the chair left the store, Jonathan said a woman came in and began speaking about a friend of hers who had experienced a long string of bad luck.

She said her friend had lost everything . . . her job, family. But, no matter what happened, no matter what she had to do, to sell, to work at to survive, that woman swore she would not give up her one prized possession . . . her hand-carved chair.

Jonathan asked what it looked like.

The customer described a chair identical to the one Jonathan had just sold.

"When she drew it on a sheet of paper," he said, "I got a chill. It was a mate to the one we had, and somewhere, now, there are two of them . . . and they are both still out there."

Don't Open the Trunk

*J*n the summer of 1973, John Pieri and two classmates who had just graduated from Coatesville Area Senior High School rented a semi-detached home on Eighth Avenue in the small southern Pennsylvania town.

The three-bedroom home was owned by an area resident, and the previous tenant, who had lived in the home for decades, had recently died.

Speaking from his present home in San Diego, California, John said, "I don't use that word. I'd say she made her transition or made her rebirth into another realm from that particular home."

A few months after moving into the building, the trio discovered a trunk in the attic. John described it as "dark, leather and wooden, with a flat top, from the 1920s or '30s."

The chest was filled with women's clothing—blouses, pleated dresses, shoes, slips, scarves, gloves, beaded pocketbooks and pillbox type hats.

"We were crazy at the time, partying and having a good time," John said. "We would go up into the attic and put on the clothes, the shoes and dresses and stuff. We were acting like we were Bonnie and Clyde, and we'd wander around the house and have a good time. Like I said, we were just crazy kids acting up, taking pictures of ourselves, stuff like that."

John said the playing around and partying with the clothing went on for about a month, then they heard the voices.

"It sounded like people were in the attic," John recalled. "From the bedrooms, we could hear voices up there and what sounded like people walking around. But when we raced up to look, it was empty. There was no one there."

Later, while they were having a barbecue in the back yard, John said, all the doors in the rear of the house, which were open, slammed shut and locked . . . by themselves.

"The back kitchen door and small shed door off of the kitchen would shut and lock by themselves. We had left them open, but we'd have to go around to the front and go in that way. That front door," John said, "didn't become locked like the others. For some reason, it was left alone, and we had to go in that way and open the back doors. And this happened more than once, it occurred several times."

The voices and noises continued, John said, then the phone calls came.

"A few times, maybe three or four, we would get telephone calls," John said. "It was an older woman asking for Jane. We told her Jane didn't live there, but she insisted that she did, that Jane had lived there for years. The caller wanted to talk to her. We said we were sorry and we didn't know what she was talking about."

John and his friends discovered that "Jane" was the name of the long-time resident who had died in the home—the owner of the trunk. The mysterious caller somehow had gotten their new phone number.

While consulting a Ouija board, John and his friends asked if there was a spirit present.

"The answer was 'Yes,' and we got goose bumps all over our bodies. Soon afterwards," John said, "we heard all sorts of noise in the attic. When we went up and looked, it was a complete wreck. Things were moved all around, in disarray. Boxes were overturned, and clothing and items were scattered all around."

The next decision was not difficult to determine or make.

"We moved the trunk out of the house," John said, "and discarded it and all of its clothing. We realized there was a spirit that was still present, and that she liked to come back and visit the place where the trunk still held her personal possessions. Being young and uninformed, we had obviously upset her by what we had been doing to her clothing.

"Sometimes, I think back to the trunk and what happened. At the time, we would laugh and thought it was all a joke. But we also were afraid, and it was spooky most of the time."

As years passed, John learned more about life and, in particular, he studied the spirit world and what occurs during the moments when the living pass on into the next realm. He believes that, years earlier, the front door probably was left alone—while the back doors were locked—because it was the portal the spirit used to enter and reenter the home during her visits.

"Back when we were 18 or 19 years old, we didn't have the understanding or the perspective that we have now," John admitted. "Knowing what I know today, I realize how we were being very disrespectful to that person's belongings and I wouldn't do it again. I would have the utmost respect of her possessions or anyone's."

Gingerbread Clock

Ken Saunders of Laura, Ohio, collects clocks—grandfather, mantle, hanging clocks—the wind-up, tick-tock types with springs and mechanical motion that depend upon human hands to provide the energy to get things moving.

He's been searching and collecting these ornate, timely keepsakes for 20 years, since he was a kid in his teens.

Timepieces using quartz mechanisms, electricity and high-tech, solar energy are of no interest to Ken.

He has about four dozen vintage clocks that he's collected through the decades from outdoor auctions. What's particularly satisfying, he said, is that he's able to repair them and get most of them working again.

"Normally, I don't have too much trouble getting them started and back to telling time," he said. "All they need is a little cleaning and oiling and they usually run fine."

But that wasn't the case with the delicately carved, turn-of-the-century Gingerbread Clock that Ken bought one weekend at an outdoor auction. It stands about 2-1/2 feet tall and has a solid metal pendulum that is suspended above the bottom of the wooden cabinet.

The wood is beautifully hand carved on the top and the sides. The pendulum is partially hidden by the highly ornamented glass door.

"I fooled with this one over two or three weeks or better, but I just couldn't get it to work," he said. "I finally just set it on the mantle, so I could admire the fine workmanship on the case."

For many months, Ken's inoperable clock served as a fine decorative addition to his collection.

Then, late one evening, while he was reading alone in his living room, the pendulum of the Gingerbread Clock began moving.

"I had owned if for about a year. I was involved in what I was reading, and I looked up and it was moving, the pendulum was swaying back and forth. There was no way it could just start up on its own. Someone or something had to pull it or push it to get it going. Then, as I was watching it swing, that metal pendulum stopped right before my very eyes. But it didn't slow down gradually. It just came down to the bottom center of the clock and . . . stopped. I didn't know what to think then, and I still don't to this day."

Over the 10 years that Ken has owned it, the clock has begun to work on its own only three or four times, and always in a different house. It has never worked twice at the same site. On the few other occasions, Ken or his wife happened to walk by the clock, and they noticed the metal disc swaying back and forth.

"We just let it go for as long as it wants to go," he said, "and when it stops, it stops. We both sort of scratch our heads. My wife and I just laugh about it and say it's our *haunted clock*. We really have no explanation for it."

Reactions to their unusual clock story, Ken said, fall into two extremes. There are those who believe in ghosts and think the incidents surrounding the clock are fascinating; and there are the others—who just roll their eyes and, as soon as possible, change the subject.

Reflecting on the incidents surrounding the antique timepiece, Ken said, "I think what intrigues me about clocks, and lamps as well, is that they were a mainstay in parlors and kitchens. At the time in history when this clock was made, there were two things that every house had, a lamp and a clock.

"Not everyone owned a piano or a certain piece of furniture, but everyone had lamps and clocks.

"During that period of time when these clocks I collect were in normal use," Ken explained, "they saw absolutely everything that happened in a house. Much unfolded in those days. Homes were where births, weddings, funerals and deaths occurred. All meals were served to the family there. No one went into town several times a day to eat at a restaurant.

"Clocks were, in a way, caretakers of human drama. They were witnesses to a lot of what went on during their time. They saw people from their cradle to the grave. If they could only talk, the stories they could tell."

The Upside-Down Rocker

iane and Mike live in an old farmhouse, outside South Paris, Maine. The attractive rural homestead has been in Diane's family since the 1890s, from the time her great-grandmother lived there.

Some say the land was the site of an army encampment during the French and Indian Wars, during the mid 1700s. As one person said, the area's as old as dirt, and dirt's been around forever. So who would ever be able to know what may have happened there.

But something apparently has been happening . . . ever since the family moved in and, more recently, when major renovations began about 20 years ago.

Diane said she and Mike have been into collecting for about eight years. They do it as a hobby, concentrating on furniture and a lot of smalls—glassware, old toys. They also inherited a lot of family heirlooms, including the Lincoln rocker, a very dark-colored piece that dates from the 1870s.

Diane explained that the chair sits very low to the floor, has a cane back and seat, and the rockers wrap up and become the chair's arm rests.

"We have no idea where it came from," she said, "but it's in very, very good condition. It looks like it has never been used, never sat in. It was up in the attic for about 40 or 50 years, until my husband brought it down a few years ago."

Diane loves the chair, she said, despite the fact that it's haunted. Her husband thinks it's the house, but she said she knows all the strange events that have happened are related to the rocker. Her mother felt the same way.

"The only time strange things happen," Diane said, "is when the rocker is stored upside down, in a position where no one can sit in it. My mother said she thought the rocking chair was haunted, and every few weeks she would go up into the attic and make sure the chair was sitting upright.

"My great-step-grandmother had always believed the rocker was haunted. She kept it in the kitchen, but wouldn't let anyone sit in it."

When Diane was growing up, her family was quite large. Between them, her mother and stepfather had eight children. After they moved into the old home, in 1974, they started to enlarge the building, adding a few rooms, winterizing and updating the major mechanical systems.

Her mother moved the Lincoln rocker into the attic to protect it from both the children and the workers. It was placed upside-down and covered, so it wouldn't be bothered.

That's when Diane first recalled strange happenings.

"We would hear something moving across the attic, after all the kids were sound asleep," Diane said. "There were footsteps, and it sounded as if someone was running across the loose floorboards."

Diane said the attic was on one end of the second floor, beside a bedroom that had a direct, walk-in entrance door.

"I remember that none of my brothers and sisters would go into the attic. Over the years, we all were assigned that adjacent bedroom and, as we've grown up and shared memories with each other, we all agree that we got weird feelings while in that bedroom."

"The chair never collected dust. You could see tiny dust particles in the sunlight, floating around in the air, but they never settled on the chair."

It was in that room, during the remodeling, that a half-dozen large pieces of sheetrock were stored, leaning up against the wall. When workers went to use them one morning, Diane recalled, the heavy, large sheets were placed flat, side-by-side, all across the floor of the empty bedroom.

"None of us kids could have done that, even as a joke. They were too heavy. After that," Diane said, "mother got really nervous and put the chair upright and left it in the attic, and the noises stopped.

"The other strange thing is that the chair never collected dust. You could see tiny dust particles in the sunlight, floating around in the air, but they never settled on the chair. Everything else in the attic was completely covered with dust, but the chair was clean. No dust settled on it. It was in extremely fine condition, it still is."

The Lincoln rocker now rests in the eerie second-floor bedroom that has been turned into a study. They've had no problems for years, but they keep the rocker upright.

"Someone definitely died on the property," Diane said, adding that she's heard stories about a man who is said to have died inside the home years ago. But she has no other clue about who, or what, causes the power that seems to come from the Lincoln rocker.

"I like it a lot," she said. "I just won't sit in it. What if the spirit decided to hurt me or do something while I was on the seat. My husband will sit in the chair. He believes in ghosts and thinks the house is haunted.

"But the rocker is surrounded by a very eerie feeling. I don't like to go into the study alone. It's almost like whatever is haunting the chair is mad when it's upside down, because it can't sit in it and rock."

Things that Go "Pop" in the Night . . . and Day

*D*on and Jimmy Walker live above a large barn, located outside Goldsboro, Maryland. It's not far from the Delaware line, about midway down the Delmarva Peninsula.

Surrounding the dark red, high-peaked structure are wandering flocks of peacocks and grazing llamas, miniature horses and Appaloosas—all part of "Walkerton," the name of the brothers' spread.

Don Walker, met us at the driveway and led us through the stall area, up the narrow wooden stairway and into a magnificent garret residence with high, A-frame ceilings and large windows that offered views of the surrounding farmland.

Throughout the large, open rooms were hundreds of antiques—collectibles, paintings, figurines, sculptures and, above all, large pieces of well-preserved, solid oak furniture.

"Oak is what we like most," Jimmy said, seated at a round oak kitchen table. "I especially like the grain of the wood."

And oak is what we were there to talk about.

The two brothers had been collecting seriously since 1986. They were dealers for awhile, and decided to concentrate on the types of pieces they liked most. When they ran out of room for display and storage, they phased out of the business end. Besides, Jimmy added, everybody was getting into the antiques business and it was becoming too overcrowded.

For years they traveled the peninsula, seeking old oak pieces.

Essentially, Don, who grooms show dogs, did the collecting and Jimmy, who works in pest control, did the stripping and refinishing.

"I drag it home, and he works on it," said Don, laughing.

When you go out West, Don said, your selection of old oak pieces is very limited, and the prices skyrocket. There's still plenty of old oak stuff on the East Coast, Don explained, because this is where people first settled and most people remained.

When some pioneering families went West and hit bad times and trouble, he said, the heavy oak furniture was the first stuff to be tossed on the side of the prairie. Much of it never made it into the Western homesteads.

About 1990, Don found something he had been seeking for years—a formal oak corner cupboard. He bought it at an auction in Cambridge, Maryland, and was told it came out of an estate in Dorchester County, on the lower Eastern Shore.

The striking piece stands at the end of the Walkers' open parlor area. Its oak body is smooth and well preserved. Arched woodwork accents the door that holds the precious antique glass, installed in the mid-1800s when the piece was made.

Standing nearly nine feet tall, it is crowned by a broken arched pediment and two original finials.

"I've had three experts look at it," said Don. "One said it was made in England, the other two thought it was American made. All agreed it was built during the 1850-60 period."

All was well in Walkerton for two weeks after the cupboard's arrival.

"Then, one day," recalled Don, "I was walking across the living room, opened the door to go downstairs to feed the horses, and I heard the loudest sound. So startling, that I turned my neck around so hard it nearly snapped."

"He nearly fell down the steps," added Jimmy, "and I flew out of my chair."

"Heavens to God," said Don, "there was this sound. The only way to describe it is this: Imagine taking a 100-pound bag filled with crystal glass, go up two stories high, turn it upside down and drop it down to a platform made of cement. The sound of all that shattering is what I heard."

"I heard the loudest sound. So startling, that I turned my neck around so hard it nearly snapped."

Jimmy jumped out of his chair and both men ran toward the cupboard, the definite source of the sound.

"I though it had fallen forward, on its ball and claw feet," Don said, "and I was going to find it face down. Then I thought maybe the top shelf had gave way and crashed to the bottom of the inside, breaking all the crystal I had placed inside.

"I tell you, it wasn't subtle. I spun my neck around so fast to see what happened, it was sore for two weeks."

In the moments afterward, Jimmy said, "We looked at each other like: *What the hell fell?* I looked at Don, and he looked back. There was nothing wrong. We checked it inside and out, and there was not one thing out of place, not one piece of glass moved."

After that came the shootings.

They started about two weeks later, with the first one in the middle of the night. To a lesser extent, they still happen, but the louder noises occurred very soon after the crystal crash.

"It sounded like a shotgun going off in the house at three in the morning," Don said. "I woke up. It was that loud. And I could sleep through a herd of elephants."

Jimmy agreed with the description. "It was definitely inside, not outside, no nearby hunters or anything like that. Absolutely not! It was as if you took a 12-gauge shotgun and fired it in this room. I jumped out of bed, I tell you."

But again, nothing out of place. No evidence of damage.

"I could sense it was a spirit," Jimmy said. "And it was a male spirit. I can tell. I've been in places where they are and I know about that stuff. I knew it was coming from the corner cupboard."

"We decided to talk to the corner cupboard," Don said. "For some reason we named him Henry. We just, literally, during daylight hours, sat here and talked openly to the corner cupboard."

Jimmy recalled his part of the conversation. "I said, 'Okay, Henry! This is enough of this crap! We aren't going to put up with it. It's got to stop.' "

Don added, "We told him, 'We like the cupboard we got. It took us four years to find it. We are not going to sell it or give it up. You may not like living above a barn, but this is our home, and we're not planning on moving out.' "

"And we're not going to part with it," Jimmy said, "and we told Henry he would have to adapt. We told him to 'Chill out!' "

After that, things calmed down. In all, the Walkers said the crashing crystal sound only occurred twice, and the shotgun blasts happened about three times.

But there still are the pops and cracks and snaps that definitely originate from the corner cupboard's area.

Jimmy said some sounds are like a .22 caliber rifle. Other pops are less strong.

Don described the sound as that of a nail popping as it's being pulled with a crowbar out of an old piece of wood.

"It may do it five or six times in a row," Jimmy said, "or one time a day. There's no way to predict.

"We've talked to people about the sounds, and they say we have to oil it, that it's the wood drying," said Jimmy. "Hell. I've done everything but grease the whole thing with enough Vaseline to shove it through a knothole, and it still does it."

There still are the pops and cracks and snaps that definitely originate from the corner cupboard's area.

Don said he's had friends over and seen them jump up off the sofa, turn and look directly at the corner cupboard when it pops.

"They look at me," Don said, "and ask if I've done anything recently to upset the ghost. We tell people about it now. It doesn't bother us to talk about it."

During the first two months, Jimmy said, "it was the really scary and unbelievable stuff. Henry's calmed down a lot now. He had us pretty upset for a while in the beginning."

But sometimes, Jimmy added, Henry won't let them unlock the glass cabinet door to get inside.

"You can put the key in," Jimmy said, "but if he don't want you in there, he won't let you in there. I don't give a damn what you want, the key just won't turn and the door can't open. Then, for no reason, after a day, a week, a few weeks, you'll try and it will just work fine."

Don said he discovered that problem when he wanted to clean the inside of the glass. The key wouldn't turn and he thought the lock had rusted inside.

"I tried '3-in-1 oil,' silicone spray, everything I could think of, and it just didn't work," Don said. "And I know I had the right key. We only have one key."

Waving his hands toward the cupboard, as if exasperated with Henry's actions, Jimmy said, "I don't fool with the damn thing. I can feel it when I get close. I just don't go near it any more. Like I said, I'm one of those people who can feel spirits, and I just back away from it now."

Intrigued by the cupboard's strange activity, Don decided to do some investigating. He contacted the auctioneer in Cambridge from whom he had bought the attractive piece that apparently serves as Henry's happy home.

After getting the name and phone number of the former owner, Don decided to try to satisfy his curiosity.

"I called him," said Don, "and told him I bought the corner cupboard at a local auction, and I asked if he could give me a brief history on it. He was very evasive, like I, literally, was a thorn in his side.

"Being the person that I am, with a direct, to the point Scorpio personality, I said, 'Okay, I know it's haunted! All I need to know is what is the problem with it, and what experiences did you have with it.'

"He said, 'You're sure it's haunted?' and I said, 'I have no doubt it's haunted.' "

Then the former owner shared his unusual experience.

The man had two sons, about 9 and 11 years old. He also had a windmill collection set up inside the corner cupboard. He kept the only key on a ring that he carried with him each day to his office.

Therefore, he was sure there was no way that the kids, or anyone else, could get into the oak cupboard.

But every day, when he returned home, he had to open the door and rearrange his antique windmills that had been moved out of place. In addition, each mill's four-cornered fan had been taken off its spindles, so they could not turn.

Don said the man told him it happened every day for two years, but that was the only problem he had with the cupboard and he could not explain it.

"After I shared the crystal and shotgun stories," said Don, "he said, 'Oh my God! Nothing that dramatic ever happened to me!' "

Don discovered that the man had purchased the cupboard from a woman who had lived for 75 years in a home in Salisbury, and before that her family had gotten it from someone in Bivalve, out on the edge of the Chesapeake Bay.

"He wasn't sure if it was made there or just from there," Don said. "Because of its features, and the time period it was made, it had to belong to someone very wealthy, maybe a governor or a person who was in some kind of official position.

"We sat and talked to Henry and tried to seek information, but we got absolutely nothing."

Jimmy said some people have told him that spirits remain in old furniture because it meant so much to the person when he was alive that he doesn't want to give it up just because he happens to be dead.

"I've talked to a number of area antique dealers about this," Don said, "and some say they've heard of it, people having haunted furniture, but they've never experienced it themselves. They say it's rare to get this kind of a haunted piece.

"But me, I'm a talker, and I tell everybody. It didn't take long for me to notice that as soon as you start talking about ghosts, you start losing people real quick. But if they don't believe me, it doesn't matter. I know what happened. The way I feel is let them try living with it for a month or two and see what they say then."

Getting up from his chair, Don walked to the cupboard, lifted the key from the drawer and stopped.

"Let's see if we can get in today," he said, smiling, holding the ornate, metal key with one hand. "I haven't tried to open it yet today."

Slowly he turned. You could hear the click of the lock. He pulled his right hand back and the door eased open.

"There you go," said Jimmy, laughing from the far side of the room, "He's in a good mood. I'd say he's generous today."

Reflecting on the cupboard's discovery and summarizing their five-year relationship with Henry, Don said, "I had been to thousands of antique shows and shops, looking for an oak piece like our corner cupboard, and I never found anything like this, so formal. Most are plain looking and made of pine and maple. So this is a one-of-a-kind find.

"I also think we've all got used to each other. We've told Henry he's welcome to stay if he settles down and doesn't make too much noise or move things around.

"The only thing is, we know no one in the family wants to inherit it. All the nieces and nephews say, *'No way!'*"

The Mysterious Victrola

Philip Bikle is an antique dealer in Huntingtown, Maryland. On the Western Shore, below Annapolis, is where he operates Bikle's Books And Collectibles.

He teaches anthropology and U.S. history at Northern Senior High School in Calvert County, but also is a part-time professor at Charles County Community College, teaching courses in the humanities.

When it comes to ghosts, Philip would be considered a skeptic, a nonbeliever, a person who would try to find the logical reason behind an action rather than simply "believe" in the supernatural. Yet today, after more than 30 years, he still has not found solid answers to events that occurred while he lived in his grandmother's home in Hagerstown, Maryland.

When Philip was 15, in the mid 1960s, his mother passed away just before Christmas. His father died two months later.

He and his younger brother moved in with their grandmother and aunt in the family home in Hagerstown. It was a large, turn-of-the-century brick house with several porches and white columns that accented the front.

Initially, the boys shared a bedroom on the second floor. But, Philip wanted a place of his own, so he moved up to one of the three rooms on the third floor.

Soon after he settled in, he heard sounds.

"They were coming up the steps and going down the hallway outside my room," Philip recalled. "It sounded like the rustling of old dresses, it was very clear and loud enough to wake me up. There also were footsteps, and they stopped right outside my door, like there was someone waiting there to come in. I thought it was my grandmother or aunt, and sometimes I'd call out, 'What do you want?' But when I opened the door, there was no one there."

Thinking it was someone playing tricks, he tied strands of dark thread in several places across the stairs and across sections of the hallway. Still the footsteps came, but when he checked the cords they were intact and had not been moved, snapped or kicked away. Whatever it was, it went over . . . or through . . . his trap.

> Thinking it was someone playing tricks, he tied strands of dark thread in several places across the stairs and across sections of the hallway. Still the footsteps came.

On some nights Philip heard voices. They sounded like someone speaking in French, in a low whisper, but he couldn't make out specific words. He thought that someone might be outside, listening to a car radio, or maybe the nails in the roof were picking up radio transmissions.

He tried to think of as many solutions as possible to the puzzling events. Eventually, he mentioned the incidents to his grandmother and aunt during breakfast.

" 'You're just imagining things,' my aunt would say. She told me to stop talking that way or I would upset my grandmother.

"But my grandmother wasn't upset," Philip said. "In fact, she said my other aunt, when she was much younger and growing up in the house as a young girl, also heard voices. But my aunt we were living with became very annoyed and told me to stop talking about this to my grandmother."

Shortly after the footsteps and whispering, Philip said he heard music coming up the stairway toward his room. He got out of bed, opened the door and followed the sound. It was coming from one of the lower levels.

When he reached the second floor landing, he met his younger brother coming out into the hallway. He, too, had heard the musical sounds.

Quietly, at two in the morning, they walked very carefully toward the sounds coming from the first-floor parlor. Standing in the darkness of the formal room was a 1920s-style RCA Victor Victrola, with its double door music cabinet and the lid at the top, shut tight.

Slowly, the two boys approached as the sounds escaped from the speaker hidden inside the dark walnut box.

"I liked playing that Victrola," Philip said, "I remember sitting in the parlor and putting on the old records that were kept in the storage racks.

"But that night, we knew it wasn't any jazz song playing. The song that we heard playing was 'Bringing in the Sheaves.' We recognized it right away. It was one they sang quite often at our church.

"What was strange is that the lid was shut. The top was down. Covering the lid was a white lace doily and a family picture was on top of that. We stared at the Victrola and we were pretty shook. We carefully opened it up, took the record off and placed it back into the storage rack."

Before they crept back upstairs, Philip took a small straight pin and placed it on top of the doily, behind the picture. He figured if anyone came and lifted the top and put a record on, the pin would be moved or fall to the floor.

"In bed that night," Philip said, "I wondered if it was all the work of my aunt. Maybe she was trying to scare us out of there. She was on a limited income and suddenly found herself caring for two teenage boys because of the death of our parents. It wasn't a situation anyone would look forward to. We were sort of a burden to her."

The next morning the two brothers returned to the parlor and approached the Victrola.

Everything was as they had left it . . . pin and all.

But Philip moved the items aside and lifted the lid.

"We looked inside. . . and the same record, from the night before, was out of the storage cabinet and back on the turntable. We looked at each other, and I accused my brother of sneaking down and pulling a trick. But he swore he didn't do it. To this day I don't know whether he did or not, but he still says he didn't put the record back in there."

A few days later Philip shared the incident with his aunt and grandmother. His aunt got emotional and told him he wasn't funny and not to mention it again.

Then she accused him of playing hooky from school and coming home in the middle of the day, disturbing his grandmother.

Philip denied it and his grandmother supported his story.

Apparently, the elderly woman had been asleep on the couch in the parlor and was awakened by two well-dressed men, who seemed to be looking around the room. She said when she asked who they were and what they wanted, the pair walked into the hall and went into the kitchen.

When Philip's grandmother got there, she said the men had disappeared. The door to the outside and the one to the cellar were locked. The men couldn't have gotten out any other way.

"My aunt began scolding me for upsetting my grandmother," Philip recalled, "but she said she was fine and that she thought the men were angels who had come for her. That was in October or November. Right before Christmas, my grandmother had a stroke and was taken to the hospital, where she died on Christmas morning. After she passed away, there were no more sounds, no more footsteps. No more music from the parlor.

"My brother lives in that house now, and he says he's never heard anything. Unfortunately, after my grandmother passed away the Victrola was sold. At that point in time my aunt was not well off, and there were dealers who came by and offered money for interesting older pieces. It's a shame, but it's gone."

When he occasionally reflects on these unusual events, Philip still wonders how they could have occurred.

Did his brother secretly go down the stairs, turn on the recording and return in time to meet him in the hallway?

Did their aunt walk the halls, whisper in French, and somehow operate the mysterious Victrola, hoping the two orphaned boys would move elsewhere?

"I'm not a believer in ghosts," Philip said. "I'm pretty skeptical about other people's stories. Had this not happened to me, I don't know what I would think. But from time to time I still wonder.

"My grandfather spent some time up in French-speaking Quebec, during the Depression, trying to make ends meet. Maybe something followed him home. Maybe he brought some object back and something else came along with it."

'Unsettling' Margaret

The moment Robert Northerner saw the haunting but beautiful portrait, he knew he would buy it. The young woman on the canvas looked so much like his wife, Carol, that the resemblance was uncanny. He could not wait to get it home to show her.

An elderly woman owned the artwork. She took a few moments to caution Robert that there was something unusual and unsettling about the portrait, but he paid no attention to her warning.

According to Robert, the documents that accompanied the painting indicate that the subject, Margaret Jeanette Keeley, was a direct descendant of the Brewster family of Massachusetts, travelers on the *Mayflower*. However, the young lady, whose father was the first justice of Massachusetts, died quite young, at 23. The painting, created by Arthur Chester, is about 3-1/2 feet square and was completed about 1840, some years after Margaret Keeley's death.

"It's painted with a mist rising from the bottom of the canvas," Robert said. "The fog seems to engulf more than half of her body, making it seem as if she's rising out of the mist. I understand it was a common practice in those days, to use such an approach when a painting was done of someone who was deceased. She is so very beautiful, with these amazing, haunting eyes."

Apparently the gaze from the subject of the portrait has affected others.

The former owner, said Robert, admitted to him that she wouldn't hang it.

"She had it wrapped in a box in the back of a closet," Robert said. "She told me her late husband said that when it was hanging the painting made him uneasy, so he took it down. After he died, his wife hung it up for a short time, but she felt the same way.

"Neither of them could get comfortable with it. The woman's husband told her he felt like someone was in the room where the painting was displayed. She agreed there was a definite presence.

"I hadn't intended to buy a painting when I went to her house, but it was so pretty, and it reminded me of my wife. I literally discovered it and bought it by accident."

Since 1987 the portrait has been in the Northerner family. A week after the artwork was hung in the second-floor hallway of their Bricktown, New Jersey, farmhouse, Robert heard the sound of a solitary violin playing a haunting, melancholy melody shortly after midnight.

At first he thought it was his imagination. Then he guessed that it was the sound from a passing car, or perhaps one that might have been parked outside, near the house, with its radio playing.

But when the music continued, Robert rose from bed, searched the house and looked outside. There was no logical source. Following the sound, he entered the second-floor guest room. As soon as he opened the door, the sound stopped.

The Keeley portrait was hanging on the wall beside the guest room doorway.

Two nights later, both Robert and Carol heard the plaintive strains of the violin. As soon as they entered the guest room, the music stopped.

Within the week, the couple was awakened by the sound of a crying child. After searching the house, they entered the guest room and the cries stopped.

From that time on, no more violins serenaded the Northerners. Instead, the sound of crying children continued for several weeks.

When these sounds stopped, they were replaced by phantom footsteps that traveled the stairs during both the day and night.

"These events occurred over a six-month period," Robert said. "If you put me under sodium pentothal, I'd swear that someone I couldn't see went up the stairs."

The Northerners attribute the unexplained incidents to the Keeley painting because the strange events in their home started almost immediately after they placed the artwork on the wall. Later, this opinion was reinforced by comments from visitors and friends.

Eventually, things settled down and no further incidents occurred. But the power of the painting never diminished.

In 1991, a middle-aged woman was house sitting for the Northerners, who, by that time, had moved to a different home.

"She got up and left in the middle of the night," Robert said. "Later, she told me that she felt that the painting, which was now hanging in our parlor, was watching her. She came back to let our dog out, by opening the door and calling it to her. But she wouldn't step foot back into the house.

"We've since asked her to house sit, and she immediately asked us, 'Is that painting still there?' When I say 'Yes,' she says she'll be back when we take it down."

> *"She told me that she felt that the painting, which was now hanging in our parlor, was watching her. She . . . wouldn't step foot back into the house."*

Another person left the house suddenly because of the powerful presence of the portrait.

"The guest said the eyes of the young woman in the painting were watching her, and she couldn't avoid them, no matter where she went," Robert recalled. "The woman said it was a captivating spell that arrested her, and it felt like the eyes of the woman in the painting were following her.

"I must admit," Robert continued, "the portrait is very arresting. There is something haunting behind those eyes. There's something there. Maybe it's because she died so young and her husband died only two years after her."

Although his family has moved several times, Robert said he always finds a prominent place in each home for the Keeley portrait.

He also has noticed a strange change of temperature near the portrait.

"When you get near the painting," he said, "it's a little bit colder. If you put your hand near the painting, you can actually feel that it's colder. It's definitely not your imagination. I have approximately 40 paintings in my house, and none has the haunting quality, and the noticeable change in temperature, like this one."

Robert often refers to the painting's unsettling qualities. He also said it seems able to draw people to it.

"If you stare at it long enough," he said, "you almost expect her to speak, she's so incredibly real. At times I even wonder if her expression changes to match the mood of the house."

Visitors and friends have made comments about the Keeley portrait.

"Usually," said Robert, "they ask, 'How can you stand that painting on the wall? We feel like it's watching us. Its presence is overpowering.'

"I just smile and don't say too much. Sometimes I mention how lovely she is, and they will agree, but then they immediately mention how much the portrait bothers them. A common comment is that they couldn't stay in the same room with it.

"Two women said there was an evil presence about the woman in the portrait that they just couldn't shake off. But I find it funny that we have so many paintings and this is the only one that seems to evoke such reactions. It really seems to have a soul of its own.

"I guess if I had to use one word to describe it, I would use 'unsettling.' The Unsettling Margaret. If you're looking for a painting to go with a setting that includes a full moon and a mist-covered night, she's the crown queen."

The Cursed Desk

Anastasia moved from Mullica Hill, New Jersey, to central Florida about 10 years ago, to operate an antique business in a 10,000-square-foot historic warehouse owned by her daughter and son-in-law.

Her new home is located between Gainesville and Lake City, in the midst of horse farms and rolling hills. It's the Florida nobody knows about, she said. Instead of surf and sand, she is nestled in the midst of what visitors and locals alike call the "Old South."

Her office and operation is in a tall, impressive, gray wooden structure that's typical of hundreds of similar buildings that dot the villages and accent the backroads throughout the region. Anastasia's particular site had been used over the last century as a storage site for gin cotton, as well as various types of grain, produce and fruits, particularly oranges.

Today the building's crop is antiques—thousands of pieces that attract endless streams of customers all year long. Anastasia specializes in period furniture, primarily upscale pieces that command a high dollar and attract a clientele that gladly pays premium prices for her fine offerings.

After dealing antiques for more than 40 years, Anastasia said matter-of-factly that she "knows her business like the alphabet."

Visitors are impressed by such finds as 150-year-old cherry and walnut sideboards, imported European armoires and 1930s era dining room and bedroom sets, all in mint condition. Oftentimes, she said, patrons have remarked: "These pieces look so perfect, you'd think they've just come out of the factory or from the craftsman's shop."

The presence of such fine furniture is probably why the old, crudely constructed, battered, pine school desk seems so out of place.

It sits in a tiny space near the warehouse front door, a reminder to Anastasia, and her regular customers, of the dealer's relationship with her close friend April.

The two women met in the summer of 1985, soon after Anastasia's arrival in the Sunshine State.

April and her husband, Ted, lived in an old plantation servant's house, located directly across the road from the furniture warehouse.

"The two of them lived frugally," Anastasia recalled. "It's believed their family came down to the Gainesville area from somewhere up in North Carolina, during the Depression.

"I would visit her often. One day, she took me into her bedroom and pointed out a school desk that she said her grandfather had made many years ago. She said it was very important to her that it be kept in the family, and, if anything happened to her, I was to make sure it was properly cared for. I didn't understand at the time, but I agreed."

Over the years, April often told Anastasia the significance of the desk. In fact, she would repeat the same story during almost every visit.

"April told me that every morning she would see a little girl, with a sad or troubled expression on her face, standing beside the old desk.

"I said it was her imagination, and that it was the sun coming in from behind the bay window with the shutters that caused a reflection and shadows," said Anastasia. "But she insisted that it was a girl standing beside the desk. April also did not like the way the little girl looked. And none of my efforts or reasoning could convince her that the apparition was not real.

"Every morning she would see a little girl, with a sad or troubled expression on her face, standing beside the old desk."

"I just passed off her remarks as unimportant and nonsensical, especially when it was discovered that April had suffered from Alzheimer's disease and was moved from her house into a nursing home. That's where she still is, to this day, and up in her late 80s, to be sure."

A few years later, in early 1990, April's husband died in their home. The couple's children removed important items and then sold everything that was left. The desk was brought to Anastasia's store to be sold, with the money going to April's nursing home care.

The desk was not in good condition. According to Anastasia, "It is not fine enough to be classified as a valuable primitive. It has a lot of scars and marks on it. The sad, lonely piece is made of several unmatched slats of wood, including a Hepplewhite style leg, and is held together with square nails."

As she prepared the desk for sale, Anastasia discovered a stack of pictures, letters, cards and mementos inside. It appeared that they had been arranged very carefully. Also, on the underside of the slant, hinged top—although quite faint because of the passing years since they were carved—she discovered the words:

> *Steal Not This Desk*
> *My Foolish Friend*
> *For Fear Thee May Die*
> *Thy End. L. Sympers—His Desk*
> *1826*

Anastasia discovered from April's relatives who still live in the county that L. Sympers was related to the family. It's assumed that April's grandfather probably had made the desk for L. Sympers. It eventually fell into April's hands, and her name is on another section of the desk.

Anastasia also found several old rocks that April had collected inside the desk.

Before closing the shop one night, Anastasia put several of them on top of the smooth writing area. The next morning, she found them on the floor.

Over time, Anastasia noticed that paper objects would not stay put on the top of the desk. They would always be discovered on the floor near the legs. Even when she taped the paper detailing the desk's history to the top of its lid, the paper would fall off.

After a while, Anastasia made it a point to check if a sudden gust of wind or nearby vibration might be the cause. But neither was ever the case. Other paper items hanging on the wall or resting nearby were undisturbed, but any material touching the desk would be moved.

In addition, Anastasia had reorganized the memorabilia within the desk after she had made the initial inspection. But, when she opened the lid the next day, the contents had been rearranged back to their original state.

"The things I left on the bottom were on the top," she said. "So I'm going to leave them that way. It seems to be the way somebody wants them."

After a few weeks, Anastasia realized that a string of bad luck seemed to strike soon after the desk's arrival.

Anastasia's car was broken into. Then there was her terrible accidental fall, followed by the expensive hospital bill.

> "I realized that since the desk came into my store, I was experiencing increasing misfortune."

An unexplained slump in business was very troublesome and, as Anastasia said, "Things that ran smoothly, just did not go smoothly at all. I realized that since the desk came into my store, I was experiencing increasing misfortune.

"I will admit that I get a very strange feeling from that particular piece. I've handled thousands of items in all my years, and I've never had this feeling before.

Well, there was this one other time, when I had a French bust. It was beautiful, but there also was something odd. I just can't explain it."

Also, Antoinette, the family cat, which is allowed to roam the warehouse at will during the day, will not go anywhere near, or crawl underneath of, April's desk.

"Virtually everybody who comes in looks at the desk," said Anastasia, "but they eventually back off. I sort of feel sorry for it. No one in the family wants it, or any of the pictures inside of it. So I'm trying to find it a decent place.

"April was just the dearest soul you would ever want to meet, and she so loved that desk. I'm just trying to do something nice for her and fulfill her wishes."

A close friend advised Anastasia to: "Get rid of that desk!" and a psychic told her: "The desk is cursed. Get rid of it!"

Trying to keep a balanced perspective, Anastasia said, "I'm not a believer in curses, nor in the supernatural, unless

I see it with my very own eyes. But, being in this business, you can't help but begin to wonder what stories these extremely old pieces that you have handled could tell.

"Some have a different feel, especially when you get the prime old pieces that have been well cared for. That poor old desk has been kicked around from pillar to post. I really hope to try to get some money for it. I must admit, though, I am becoming aggravated with all this aggravation . . . .

"But, what am I supposed to do? I promised April that I would take care of it for her. I guess I'll just have to wait for the right person to come along and take it away to a good home. But if you learn anything in this business, it's that you've got to be patient."

Where There's Smoke,
There's . . . a Ghost

harron Cypher has been an antique dealer for
more than 20 years. She still operates Sharron's
Antiques in Hartford, Wisconsin, where her spe-
cialty is large case pieces, including cupboards and
wardrobes.

Sharron also lived for more than seven years with poltergeists and spirits in an old Wisconsin farmhouse. So she can
fill a book with the events she and her family have not only
witnessed but lived through.

Perhaps that's why she can relate the strange incidents
surrounding her Wisconsin, black walnut, jelly cupboard in
such a comfortable, casual, matter-of-fact tone. It may not be
everyone's reaction to unexplained events, but it certainly is
Sharron's.

It was in 1980, up in nearby Fond du Lac County, that
Steven and Sharron purchased an 1850s era, flat-topped jelly
cupboard. It stood about 5 feet high and 4 1/2 feet wide.

It had a set of blind doors that covered the low, enclosed
shelves and was made for storing canned goods and food-
stuffs preserved in old, short glass jars.

They had used it to store books, but, Sharron said, after
about three years they found a large Victorian bookshelf for
that purpose and took the jelly cupboard to a weekend
antique sale at a Ramada Inn in Milwaukee.

Usually, overnight security is provided, Sharron said.
Since this was the first time the dealers were conducting
their own event, the participants split up the security duties.

Late Thursday night, after the show was set up, Sharron
and Steven's friend Larry, who was the husband of another

dealer, had fallen asleep on a plank table not far from their booth.

"He had dozed off," Sharron said, "and when he woke up, he thought our booth was on fire. He said there was smoke everywhere. He ran to see what he could do, to contain it on his own, but he couldn't find anything. He saw smoke, but there were no flames, no smell and no heat.

"All of the sudden, while he was standing right in front of the booth, he saw all the smoke turn into a stream and disappear into the jelly cupboard."

"While he was standing right in front of the booth, he saw all the smoke turn into a stream and disappear into the jelly cupboard."

Sharron said Larry was all alone and the incident occurred at three in the morning. Not surprisingly, he didn't get any more sleep that night. He stared at Sharron's booth until morning, thinking the fire—or smoke or whatever it was—might start up again.

"When we arrived the next morning, on Friday," she said, "he was practically scared to death! He was so animated he was hysterical.

"After all we'd been through, with ghosts and poltergeists and unusual occurrences at our house, my husband and I don't consider anything really outlandish or strange. And since the cupboard had been taken out of our house, that was filled with spirited activity at the time, we just laughed about the whole thing.

"Larry said, 'I have to get home to get some sleep,' then he added, 'It's got to be one of your ghosts.'

"All of our friends knew we were living with a lot of them," Sharron explained.

On Friday night and for the rest of the show, there was no more trouble. On Saturday morning, they found out why.

Early Saturday morning, Larry's wife came in and told Sharron that late Friday night, when Larry got up to go to the bathroom, she saw the full figure of a man walking behind Larry in the darkness of the room.

She said it was not smoky, but a light outline that you could only see in the darkness. When he turned on the bathroom light, it disappeared from view. It was exactly Larry's size and shape, and walked or drifted right behind him.

"Apparently," Sharron said, "whatever had been living in the jelly cupboard went home with Larry and lived with him for several months."

Larry's wife told Sharron that her husband never saw the figure, because it always walked behind him. Also, when he tried to see it by looking in the mirror, he could not see a figure.

"She told me," said Sharron, "that she became so used to seeing it that, after a while, she wasn't even shocked. Then, all of the sudden, she found herself looking for Larry's spirit friend, and he was gone. That's when she realized he wasn't there anymore."

Sharron added that the jelly cupboard had been in her shop for three years, and no one had ever bothered to look at it.

"Then, when the smokey spirit friend went home with Larry," Sharron said, "we sold it immediately at the show. It was like whatever it was must have been happy living at our place and didn't want to be disturbed. So it was holding people back, keeping them away from buying it."

The Antique Copper Bathtub

or two years, immediately after they retired, Jane and Ben spent their free time collecting antiques. Every weekend, evening and holiday they would set out in their van and hit the auctions and flea markets throughout Tennessee, Alabama and Kentucky.

After a short time, their two-bedroom apartment was overflowing with furniture and collectibles—all original and authentic pieces for their newly built log cabin, located on the outskirts of Pulaski, Tennessee.

"It was while the cabin was under construction," recalled Ben, "that we were walking through a flea market in Nashville and saw an antique bathtub. We both stopped, looked at each other and said, at the same time, 'That's the one!' "

They bought the six-foot long, wood encased, copper-lined tub and had the dealer deliver it to their apartment.

"It was in good shape," said Ben. "The wooden body and copper lining were smooth and clean. It had a drain and overflow, and there was no rotten wood or bugs. To tell you the truth, we were looking for something that would fit into the new cabin, and it seemed like the perfect thing. We stored it upright in one of the bedrooms in the apartment. Honestly," Ben paused to let out a laugh, "it sorta looked like a coffin."

Neither Ben nor Jane had any idea about the age of the bathtub.

For insurance purposes, Ben photographed each new antique he and Jane acquired. As he did with all their other pieces, Ben took two photographs of the tub and sent them in to be developed at Kroger's, a large supermarket and pharmacy near their home.

When the roll was developed, Ben tossed the pictures into a box. He usually waited until he had a few packets of photos and then went through them as a group.

"When I looked through the packets, I didn't come across any pictures of the tub," Ben said. "I thought I took pictures of the tub, but then I wasn't sure. I didn't know if they didn't come out or if I just forgot and never took them."

When the next roll of film was in the camera, Ben made sure he took pictures of the tub. In fact, they were the last two shots on the roll.

"This time I accidentally opened the camera and exposed the last two shots on the roll, so the pictures of the tub didn't turn out. But I wasn't concerned and didn't think anything was wrong, so on the next roll of film I made sure that the first two pictures I took were of the tub."

When this roll of film was returned, everything except the two shots of the tub turned out.

"Now I'm really upset," said Ben, "and I'm thinking I'm going to get a picture of this tub. I'm getting obsessed to get a picture of the thing. So I take out a new roll and I take 15 pictures of the bathtub. I shot it from every angle I could get.

"When that film came back, I opened it up in the store and took a quick look at two or three of the shots. Finally, I had gotten pictures of the bathtub."

Later when Ben got home, he looked at the entire pack of photographs.

All of the pictures he took of the tub turned out, even the ones where Jane was standing in front of the upright, coffin-like box.

But, he explained, for two of the shots he had posed in front of the tub and Jane took his picture with the antique. In that pair of pictures there was an obvious mist or haze.

"In one shot I was pretending to be bathing," Ben said. "In the other I was standing with my arm out, around some invisible being. I remember joking that this was the fourth roll of film we had used to get a picture of the tub and maybe the reason for the picture problems is that we have a bashful ghost.

"In the picture, it looks like my arm is around somebody and there is a definite haze or fog coming from the tub that almost obliterates me."

Although Ben said he isn't one to believe in ghosts or spirits, he showed the picture to some of his former coworkers. To his amazement, they all agreed there is something mysterious about the tub and the misty haze.

Ben said that after the photograph controversy, his wife refused to allow him to install the tub in their bathroom. Instead, they bought a metal, ball and claw foot Victorian bathtub for their house.

The copper antique remains in one of the bedrooms, resting flat on the floor against one wall with an old door stretching across the top and covering the copper interior.

"I use it for stacking my tools. It's really turned into a very nice workbench," Ben said. "Jane said she will not have it hooked up in her house, period. She said, 'You can't drown in a tub that isn't connected and isn't able to hold any water.' And I've found her reasoning isn't that unusual. Whenever I mention this story to anyone who is connected with the spiritual world, they suggest that someone may have died or drowned in the tub. And I've heard that from more than one person."

Living in a log cabin, and admitting that he has some odd habits and quirks, Ben said he knows he seems a bit eccentric to others. Therefore, he hasn't told the story to too many people.

In fact, he had tried to keep it from his grandchildren. But, one day when six-year-old Anthony was visiting with his two older cousins, the youngster discovered the photograph of Ben, beside the tub and surrounded by the mist.

"Without even knowing the story," said Ben, still amazed at the occurrence, "little Anthony calmly set down the picture, looked at me and said, 'It's haunted.' Then he walked off to play."

Ben has tried to think of a logical reason for the initial problems with the pictures not turning out and then the mist appearing in his photographs. His only explanation is that, perhaps, the large amount of copper caused a reaction that

"Without even knowing the story, little Anthony calmly set down the picture, looked at me and said, 'It's haunted.'"

ruined the film. But, that doesn't explain why the photos of his wife turned out and the ones of him were hazy.

"I just don't know," he said. "Nothing really surprises me. My wife tends to lean towards the haunting, and I lean the other way, because I'm sort of skeptical about this.

"To tell you the truth," Ben said, lowering his voice and sounding as if he was sharing a secret, "I really have kept most of what occurred to myself, and I'll tell you why.

"Do you remember when you were a kid and there was an old haunted house in the neighborhood? It was old and spooky looking. And on a Friday night you and your friends would all get together and sneak up there to look around. And you'd all point at the people who lived there and say: 'They're the ones.'

"Well, now, I'm the one. But because I had you change my name in this story, they're never going to know about me or find out exactly who I am."

The Anniversary Ring

or several years in the 1980s, I lived in a small, quiet development. It was made up of a few hundred townhouses and single homes, plus several apartment buildings, in Maryland, about a half mile west of the Delaware line.

Its only entrance was off Delancy Road, a narrow side road that feeds onto old U.S. Route 40, a four-lane highway that is born near the surf of Atlantic City, New Jersey, and dies in the Old West near Heber City, Utah.

Until the 1970s, farm fields dominated the landscape on most of both sides of Delancy Road, except for a few small homes scattered here and there.

I lived in a three-bedroom row home for three years. It was well built, spacious, comfortable, convenient to shopping and work . . . and, well, actually, a bit strange.

My son and I would sometimes ask each other who had shut certain doors, who had been walking in the middle of the night or what was the cause of unexplained sounds. Also, my bedroom was always exceptionally cold, in both summer and winter, while the rest of the house responded to the temperature setting on the thermostat.

We never found any definitive answers to our concerns, which I must add were never the cause of any great worry. Rather, they were minor annoyances that could not be resolved or understood.

About three years after I moved out, I received a telephone call from Tom. He explained who he was—a former neighbor who I would often see working in his yard when I walked my dog. We had become passing neighborhood friends, a quick wave, a brief hello, a bit of small talk and not much more. We both understood the unspoken rules of the relationship and on both sides that was fine.

Tom asked to speak to me. He also had moved from the development, read that I was writing about ghosts in the area and told me he had a tale to tell. Nothing more than that.

A few days later, I met him in the Howard House restaurant in the center of Elkton. After a quick handshake, we settled back in our chairs—in a corner out of earshot of any other patrons—Tom gave a few quick glances to the right and left, then said:

"You're not going to believe this, but I've got to tell somebody who will not think I'm crazy."

I nodded and told him I've heard the same statement almost every time someone is ready to share a ghost story.

He shook his head in agreement, happy that I had recognized his concern. Then he got into it.

Tom reminded me of where he had lived, in a corner townhouse that was close to an open field and a clump of trees. He and his wife bought it so they could have more privacy than living in an interior unit. Also, he was down a block or two from the entrance, so there wasn't too much traffic.

He said he liked to do handyman stuff around the house and outside, could never sit still.

I nodded, telling him I recalled the deck he had built and the bird feeders and the shed . . . .

"That's what started it all," he said, almost snapping, "that damn shed!"

It was in late summer of 1993 when Tom decided to build a shed. Rather than throw down a load of gravel and have a pre-built model dropped off, he was going to build his own, complete with concrete footers and an air vent area underneath.

To get the holes dug below the frost line took a little doing, and he needed to go down about three feet.

"I like to work alone," Tom said. "It's like therapy to me. I work all week at the Christiana Mall, in retail sales. Sometimes, it drives me crazy with all those people running back and forth. I do this stuff to relax and get away from it all. So nobody else was around when it happened."

"What happened?"

He was working on the third footer, in the farthest end of his yard, near the rose garden, when he shoveled up a ring.

"It was beautiful," he said, his mind remembering the pale white opal in the center surrounded by seven dark blue stones.

"I couldn't believe it. It had to be about a foot below the ground. I first saw it in the pan of the shovel, catching the sun and sparkling. I rested the shovel down very carefully. I didn't want to lose it. Then I went over to pick it up from the dirt . . . but . . . ."

Tom paused, started wringing his hands, and took a sip from his beer.

"Look," he said, "I want you to know this is hard for me. I know I shouldn't have done it. And if I was to do it over, I'da called the cops, but . . . you have to understand."

"I'm not here to make judgments, just to listen."

"Okay." He took another swallow from the brown long-neck, then rubbed the bottle back and forth between his two palms. "You have to promise not to tell anybody who I am. You can tell the story, but not my name. Understand?"

"Fine. I'll change your name. Most people want me to do that anyway. It's not unusual. Okay?"

"All right, 'cause people should know."

"Know what?" I asked.

"About what's there . . . ."

I waited in silence. Then he continued.

"Anyway, I went to pick up the ring that was peeking through the top of the dirt in the shovel, and, as I grabbed it, there was. . . ." He started to whisper. "There was a bone, a bunch of thin finger bones, hanging through the round, bottom part of the ring."

Tom went on, saying how he looked around, stuffed the ring in his pocket, and sifted through the shovel looking for more bones, more rings, anything. He then went back into the hole and dug deeper and to the sides, but much more carefully than before. He eventually dug down more than four feet and made a crater about three feet across.

"I found a few more human bones, tiny ones," he said, "So I figured that must be the rest of the hand. Nothing else.

"I didn't know where it came from. Nobody saw me. I was so excited about that ring that I didn't even think of calling the cops or asking around. Besides, I guess I figured that if I told anybody I'd have to give the ring back. I wasn't thinking right."

I waited for him to continue, but in the silence he got upset.

"Do you think I did wrong? Huh?"

"Look, Tom. I'm only here to listen. I don't know what I would have done in that situation. Who does? Relax. So what happened next?"

He said he filled the area back in, except for the spot needed for the footer, then he took the handful of bones and tossed them into the center of the hole. That afternoon, he poured concrete into all four spots and buried the bones in footer number three.

"Our anniversary was coming up in only a week," Tom said. "It was rough at work, sales were way off. When you work on a low salary and rely on commissions, sometimes it's really bad. I didn't have any money for a gift for Janice, so I got a box from a jeweler friend at the mall. He didn't ask any questions. I put the ring in a box, wrapped it up and gave it to her a week later.

"She knew times were tough and said she would have been fine with just a card. I tell you, though, she was thrilled.

"But soon afterwards, just a day or two, the dreams started."

"Within a week of receiving the ring, Janice started waking up in the middle of the night, first shouting, then screaming. Rambling on about this dream."

Within a week of receiving the ring, Tom said, Janice started waking up in the middle of the night, first shouting, then screaming. Rambling on about this dream, the same one every night.

She told him there were two people, seated in a bus or train, side by side. The woman was very beautiful, young and stylish. The husband the same. In their mid 30s. The lady in the dream was holding the man's hand and always asked the same question: "How long before we get there?"

"Before he can answer her," said Tom, "Janice says there's a bright, yellow flash that appears and she hears screaming. And then my wife wakes up screaming. It got to the point where she started taking sleeping pills. But they didn't help. Then she tried to stay up all night and not go to sleep at all."

In the midst of the second week, Janice started hearing whispers in the house, and outside in the yard. At first, she thought it was saying, "Where's my thing" or "I want my thing."

After ignoring it for several days, Janice started talking to the voice, and shouting out "Who are you?" and "What do you want with me?"

The voice would repeat the same phrase, up to a dozen times a day, "I want my thing."

"She was going nuts," Tom said. "I was losing it, too. I knew the voice was crazy, and I had figured it wanted the ring. But there was no way I could tell her. Then she would know where I got it. All hell broke loose when she started telling her friends."

Janice had lost weight, started smoking again and looked totally wasted, like an alcoholic on a constant binge. Her friends noticed her state and, during a coffee session in Janice's kitchen one morning, someone suggested that the voice might be calling for the "ring."

Looking at the opal and blue jewels on her hand, Janice gasped. As soon as Tom came home, she demanded that he tell her how he had gotten it and where it had come from.

"I lied," he said, shaking his head. "I had to, told her it came from a pawn shop. What could I do, say, 'Yeah! I took the ring off a dead woman buried in our back yard'? No way. She would have killed me. I figured I could ride it out a little longer and it would all go away. Boy, was I wrong."

With the dreams continuing, and the anniversary gift now suspect, the voices continued. Janice had placed the ring back in the box. The end came when the phone calls started.

"I swear," Tom said, "I couldn't believe it. The phone rang, I was right there, and she answered it. Then she started screaming and fell to the floor huddled up in a ball. The phone was swinging from the cord on the kitchen wall.

"Janice was babbling, pointing and shaking toward the phone. I picked it up and shouted 'Hello! Who is this?'

"As God is my witness," Tom paused, took another sip of beer. "I get chills just thinking about it. I tell you, I heard it. It was a woman's voice, and . . . ." Tom's lips were shaking as he whispered the words, "she said, 'I want my ring back!' Those were her exact words.

"I slammed down the phone and grabbed Janice. I told her it was a joke, probably one of her stupid friends that was trying to scare her. But she wasn't listening. She was in shock, really shaking. Man, I mean she wouldn't stop. I shook her. Slapped her across the cheeks. I was starting to freak out. I almost called the ambulance, but I got her a drink, took her up to bed and tucked her in.

"She was clinging to me, her fingers and nails digging into my arm. I felt like crap. She was afraid to sleep, afraid to stay awake.

"I told her I'd take the ring back to the store. Get rid of it. I still couldn't tell her the truth. I figured if I got it out of the house, things would stop, settle down, anyway. Another mistake."

A few days later, Tom took the ring to a pawnshop in Baltimore. Got over a hundred bucks and drove back home. He said he figured it would become somebody else's problem now.

He was both right and wrong.

Even though the phone calls stopped, Janice was still having the dream. By then, she was going to counseling. The whispers were less frequent, but still happened. Tom said he and Janice were at each other's throats all the time. She wasn't doing anything around the house. It was a mess. She was smoking and drinking.

"I started hitting the bottle, too," he admitted. "It was the only way to get through the night. When the phone rang, we wouldn't answer. We let the answering machine screen the calls, we were worried it would be 'The Voice.' This must sound nuts, but it gets worse."

"Go on," I urged him.

"The whole thing really exploded before the end of the year."

"What happened?"

He shook his head in disgust and slammed his bottle onto the table. "One of her damn friends brought over a copy of the *Neighborly News*, the neighborhood newsletter. The headline read: 'Elkton Was Site Of Airplane Tragedy.' It happened in December of '63. Over 80 people were killed when the plane was struck by lightning over the town. The plane crashed in the fields off Delancy Road, where some say houses are now.

"The story said they closed the road for a week, picking up scraps of the plane, and luggage and other stuff was all over the place. There were so many holes in the area, that people used to call it 'Crater Road.' The newsletter said the residents were talking about placing a marker to commemorate the 30th anniversary of the crash.

"I walked in the door, and Janice was waiting for me. She and her friends had figured I must have found the ring in the fields or something, and it was haunted.

"You gave me a dead woman's ring!' she screamed. She was throwing things at me. Tearing up the place. It was a wreck. Stuff was broken all over the house, furniture tossed around. She had her bags packed. I couldn't even explain. She walked out on me."

Tom stayed in the house alone. Janice filed for divorce. He got the papers from her lawyer and had to pay for her counseling.

"So I'm there alone, and then the dreams and voices start on me. I mean, it was constant. Some nights I'm out in the parking lot, sleeping in my car. By now the house is a wreck, inside and out. I look like a nut. The neighbors are staring at me like I'm insane.

"I decided I've got to put the ring back. Then everything will be okay. So I drive to Baltimore, to the pawnshop, to buy it back. When I get there, the lady remembers me. I mean, how many people in the city remember somebody who came into a pawnshop months before?

"But she was getting bad dreams, the same ones, about the couple talking before the bright flash."

"It seems that everybody who touched the ring was having the same dreams."

The pawnbroker gave Tom the name of the person who bought the ring, and he drove out and knocked on the door.

"I thought they would think I was nuts, but the husband lets me in and, within minutes, he brings me the ring, in a box and says take it. He didn't even want any money for it. It seems that everybody who touched the ring was having the same dreams. It was freaky, I tell you."

Tom took the ring home, planning to put it back.

"But I couldn't put it back on the finger. You see, I had buried the bones in the cement," he shook his head slowly. "I even thought of moving the shed and trying to break up the concrete footer and trying to find the bones, but decided that was really nuts. I put it in a plastic bag and buried it deep in the rose garden, about two feet down, as close as I could to the footer where the finger bones were. That's the best I could do."

Apparently, it wasn't good enough. Both the dreams and the whispers continued. Eventually, Tom moved in with his brother and put the vacant house up for sale.

"I was even afraid to go over there alone to clean it up and cut the grass," he said.

I asked if he told the real estate agent about the voices and strange events.

"No way! Do you think I was nuts? It was hard enough to sell the house as it was, vacant, going through a divorce. If I said anything about the ring and voices, it would have been the kiss of death. Besides, the way I figured it, as long as they didn't find the ring and didn't touch it the new owners would be fine."

Finally, in the summer of 1994, Tom said he made settlement on the house. Everyone was agreeable at the lawyer's office. Unfortunately, he forgot to bring the extra set of keys and arranged to drop them off later that afternoon.

When Tom arrived at his old home, the young family was moving in. Boxes, furniture and toys were scattered across the small front lawn.

Looking up at the house, Tom said he made an effort to push the horrifying experiences that had occurred there from his mind. Trying to remain calm, he shook the new owner's hand and wished him well. As Tom turned to walk toward his car, he tripped over a bright blue bag resting on the sidewalk. The word "White's" was written across the top in white script lettering.

"Almost as a reflex, I don't know why, but I asked him what it was. He knelt down and unzipped the vinyl case. 'It's my metal detector,' he said, adding that he was addicted to the thing. He said the first thing he does when he goes anywhere is check out the area."

Tom said his mind and body froze. He recalled being unable to move.

98

"Then the guy held the machine up in front of my face and said, 'This baby will give you a signal down to about three feet. Isn't that something?'

"I was still in shock," Tom said. "I think I told him that it was great or something like that. Then, the last thing I remember him saying as I was walking away—I didn't even turn back and look at him—and he shouted, 'There's more gold in the ground than there is in the banks!'"

—Ed Okonowicz

Author's Note: This story is fiction. However, in the *Guinness Book of World Records*, the town of Elkton, Maryland, is mentioned under the heading: "Worst Disasters in the World." On Dec. 8, 1963, lightning hit a Pan American 707 as it was heading toward a landing in Philadelphia's airport. It is the worst recorded disaster resulting from a lightning strike: all 81 people died—73 passengers and eight crew members.

Years later, developments of single homes, townhouses and apartments were built near the crash site. Some area residents have heard stories, and others claim to have seen lost souls, walking through the yards and along the area streets and sidewalks. Others say they have heard of people who claim to have seen the hazy outlines of sad faces that seem to stare out from the flames of home fireplaces.

But most say all the talk is only rumor and superstition.

A memorial plaque, commemorating the 30th anniversary of the crash and recovery operation, was dedicated during a formal, memorial ceremony in the spring of 1994.

Perhaps that community remembrance of the tragedy of more than 30 years before will allow any troubled, wandering souls to finally rest in peace.

About the Author

E d Okonowicz, a Delaware native, is a freelance writer for local newspapers and magazines. Many of his feature articles have been about ghosts and spirits throughout the Delmarva Peninsula. He is employed as an editor and writer at the University of Delaware, where he earned a bachelor's degree in education and a master's degree in communication.

Also a professional storyteller, Ed is a member of the National Storytelling Association and several regional storytelling organizations. He presents programs at country inns, retirement homes, schools, libraries, public events, private gatherings, birthday parties, Elderhostels and theaters in the mid-Atlantic region.

He specializes in local legends and folklore of the Delaware and Chesapeake Bays, as well as topics related to the Eastern Shore of Maryland. He also writes and tells city stories, many based on his youth growing up in his family's beer garden–Adolph's Cafe–in the Browntown section of Wilmington, Delaware. He tells tales about the unusual characters each of us meet in our everyday lives.

Ed presents beginning storytelling courses and also writing workshops based on his book *How to Conduct an Interview and Write an Original Story.*

About the Artist

athleen Burgoon Okonowicz, a watercolor artist and illustrator, is originally from Greenbelt, Maryland. She studied art in high school and college, and began focusing on realism and detail more recently under Geraldine McKeown. She enjoys taking things of the past and preserving them in her paintings.

Her first full-color, limited-edition print, "Special Places," was released in January 1995. The painting features a stately stairway near the Brandywine River in Wilmington, Delaware.

A graduate of Salisbury State University, Kathleen earned her master's degree in professional writing from Towson State University. She is currently a marketing analyst at the International Reading Association in Newark, Delaware.

Her childhood bear, "Pinkie Whitey," who appears on the cover of this book, has a haunting tale of his own. The *spirited* bear managed to survive a fire that totally destroyed all the other contents of the attic in which he resided. Days after the fire, he was found amidst the charred rubble, unsinged and unscorched, not even smoked-damaged. "That's my bear!"

The couple resides in Fair Hill, Md.

$\mathscr{S}$pirits $\mathscr{B}$etween the $\mathscr{B}$ays
Series

by Ed Okonowicz
"The Delmarva Peninsula's Stephen King..."
WILMINGTON NEWS JOURNAL

Volume I

Pulling Back the Curtain

The first book in a series of true ghost stories.
Relive 8 real-life ghostly experiences and enjoy
2 local legends.

$8.95   *"A treat from professional storyteller Okonowicz."*

INVISIBLE INK
ghost catalog

64 pages   5 1/2 x 8 1/2 inches   softcover   ISBN 0-9643244-0-7

Volume II

Opening the Door

13 more true-life Delmarva ghost tales and one
peninsula legend.

*" 'Scary' Ed Okonowicz ... the master of written
fear—at least on the Delmarva Peninsula ...
has done it again."*
WILMINGTON NEWS JOURNAL

$8.95

96 pages   5 1/2 x 8 1/2 inches   softcover   ISBN 0-9643244-3-1

TRue
Ghost Stories
from the
master storyteller

Volume III

Welcome Inn

Features true stories of unusual events in
haunted inns, restaurants, and museums
". . . a sort of auto-club guide to
ghosts, spirits and the unexplainable . . . ."

$8.95
Theresa Humphrey, ASSOCIATED PRESS
story in THE WASHINGTON TIMES

96 pages   5 1/2 x 8 1/2 inches   softcover   ISBN 0-9643244-4-X

Volume IV

In the Vestibule

$9.95
Tales of suspense drift beyond the bays, to the
Jersey shore, Philadelphia and Baltimore
suburbs and, of course, back into Delmarva.

Coming in the Fall of 1996

If you're left craving for more, well . . .
we haven't finished yet.

Coming soon

Possessed
POSSESSIONS 2

More Haunted Antiques, Furniture
and Collectibles

Featuring:

The Vaudeville Doll
Clothing with Spirit
Who Do Voodoo?
Civil War Ambrotypes
The Pesky Piano
The Cursed Crib
A Revolutionary War Painting
Mirror Mirror on the Wall

Plus Stories Submitted by You
(see form on page 106 to share your experience)